WORKING WOMEN
IN SOUTH AFRICA

For all the women whose experiences fill the pages of this book
– and especially for
Agnes, Alfie, Alice, Annah, Catherine, Connie, Dolly, Elizabeth, Elsie, Emma, Flora, Gugu, Joan, Kate, Liza, Louise, Mabel, Ma Dlomo Lugogo, Mam' Lydia, Mary, Margaret, Maureen, Mildred, Miriam, Nora, Olive, Pam, Pauline, Stephanie, Thembi.

WORKING WOMEN IN SOUTH AFRICA

Lesley Lawson for the Sached Trust

Pluto Press

Text and photographs by Lesley Lawson

Edited by Helene Perold
Designed by Mary Anne Bähr and Ray Carpenter
Artwork by Pamela Goller
Typesetting by Opus 61

First published by Ravan Press (Pty) Ltd and the Sached Trust, South Africa 1985
This edition published in 1986 by Pluto Press Limited,
The Works, 105a Torriano Avenue, London NW5 2RX
and Pluto Press Australia Limited, PO Box 199, Leichhardt,
New South Wales 2040, Australia. Also Pluto Press,
27 South Main Street, Wolfeboro, New Hampshire 03894-2069 USA

Copyright © The Sached Trust 1985, 1986

7   6   5   4   3   2   1

90   89   88   87   86

Printed in Great Britain by The Alden Press, Oxford

British Library Cataloguing in Publication Data
Lawson, Lesley
    Working Women in South Africa.
    I. Women, Black – South Africa – Social conditions
    I. Title   II. Sached Trust
    305.4'88968   HQ1800.5

ISBN 0 7453 0206 8

Contents

Rose Modise

Rose Modise has been a factory worker for over twenty years. Her life story sums up the problems that a working woman faces — both at work and in the home.

I was born in Soweto and I grew up in Soweto. In 1967 I got married. I had three children. One passed away and two are still alive.

I left school after Standard Six. My father was dead long ago and my mother couldn't afford to keep us at school. My brother and I had to look for jobs. I was seventeen.

I had two brothers. My eldest brother was a soldier in the war (Second World War). He even went to Egypt. When he came back he was crippled. He had been shot.

I got a job at a factory. I worked there for five years. You know what they paid me? £2 10s every week! That was around 1962.

At that time I was staying with my mother. My younger brother was also staying there. He worked for a record company for £10 a week. That was a high wage then.

On Fridays I came home with the money I earned, closed in a very small envelope, and I gave it to my mother. My brother also gave her his wage. She used to give us three shillings or something every day.

There were mainly women working at this factory. The women were labourers. The men who worked there were operators. It wasn't heavy work. I was just wrapping these things.

One day I went to talk to the production manager. I told him that the money was too little. I told him my mother was not working, and we must pay rent and everything. Then I was fired. I had been working there for five years without an increase!

The women were not meant to be operators, only men. The women never got promoted. We worked for £2 10s because there was no other work to do. Women felt it was better to get £2 10s than nothing.

It's still like this today. Women are getting very little — especially factory women, garment workers. I know this woman who is getting R26 a week. And her husband is not working because he was not born here. He is a migrant worker and he can't get a job.

We people manage because we live on cheap food. Not because we don't like to eat the best, but because we can't afford it. Sometimes I'd like to buy a packet of rice, but I buy mealie meal instead. It's offal instead of steak — because you need the money to live for the week.

Anyway, after I was fired from that place I got a better job. I told the new manager I was getting £10 a week in the last job. So he gave me £16. I was lucky. I have stayed in this same job ever since. It's a paper factory.

Soon I got married. My husband was a teacher. We had a house in Meadowlands then. Just my husband and I. We were lucky to get a house — it was because he was a teacher and working for the government. If you work for the government you get housing quicker.

It is hard being a working mother. With my first baby I stopped work a week before she was born. They said if I wanted my job back I must stay away only six weeks. And that six weeks was mixed with

Steam ironing in a Johannesburg knitwear factory (1981)

my leave. So I had to take my baby to an old lady during the day.

Let's say it's Monday and I had to go to work. I had to wake up at four o'clock, because I had to wash the nappies I'd been using during the night. The old lady wouldn't take dirty nappies.

Then, make food for the baby, take the baby on my back and drop her with the old lady, come back, take the other child — the clever one — halfway to school.

I had to take my child very early to school because I had to be early at work. School only started at 8.30 a.m. but at 6.30 a.m. my baby was there. I always took her. It was far too dangerous for her to go by herself.

There was never time for me to make coffee for myself or for my husband. I was busy from the time I woke up at four o'clock.

I used to catch the train at about 6.20 a.m. to be at work at 7.30 a.m. The train was full already because I caught it in the middle of Soweto. We'd have to stand for almost forty-five minutes. We had friends on the train and we talked all the way — "Hey I was late" — and things like this. The trains never emptied. When you came to a station you'd have to move out to let them off. When five got out, ten got in. Until Johannesburg.

When I got to work I'd make coffee for myself. Just pinch a little time. After this coffee, then start work. But it was nice because we were used to it. We used to sing sometimes if we were happy. We didn't care about anything.

The day that made us fed-up was Friday. Just Friday. Because Friday is the day when you start thinking about your 'cracks' (*debts*). "I owe somebody such and such, I'm getting so little money. I have to pay the lady who looks after my baby, I must buy coal..." When you start calculating the wages you find by Saturday morning you are empty. People always do that on a Friday — paying debts.

I used to knock off at 4.30 p.m. and reach Soweto by 6 p.m. In winter it's dark at that time. I had to go straight home and then fetch the baby from the old lady. The bigger one could come home by herself. After that I'd make the fire and start to cook — one or two pots. Cooking took till 8 p.m. or 8.30 p.m. And the poor kids — they were already sleeping. Sometimes I'd wake them up and then they wouldn't eat well, because they were drowsy. Sometimes they didn't even eat — they just slept. In the morning I might have time to make them tea.

My husband came home from school at 3 p.m. or 3.30 p.m. He'd just sit around with his pile of books — correcting books or something like that. Sometimes he'd make the fire. He wouldn't cook. He said he was not a woman. We used to fight about that because when I was sick he did cook.

He could cook. I remember one day I came home — it was winter time — and I smelt the smell of nice soup. He was happy. He said: "Have a taste, don't even sit down." He gave me this tasty soup. Then only I had to go and bath the babies. It was simple.

When he didn't do anything I used to feel cross. Sometimes I'd come home and he was still somewhere drinking.

It's really tough being a working wife. I was worried about my babies. That old lady was really old. One old lady and a bunch of six babies! Sometimes she'd give them sour milk. Sometimes one would take the other one's bottle, because he's hungry and he couldn't find his own. Sometimes I'd talk to the old lady saying, "This milk you give my child doesn't seem fresh, but I'm bringing you fresh milk every morning." And she'd say, "No, but I can't afford all these children." And I would say, "But I'm paying you!" She wanted the money so she didn't send any children away.

I always think that's why my baby died. She had gastro-enteritis. They said she was getting the wrong kind of food. I always blame that work, because I had no time to stay with my kids. That was my last baby.

And when you are a working wife you don't give your kids the right morals. Your kids get spoilt because you let them run around by themselves. They can even pinch. You miss too much of them — you only see them at night. Sometimes you don't see them at all because when you get home they're sleeping already.

That's part of neglecting your kids. Because as a woman, you've got to be with your kids and stay with them. I did want to give up work, but I couldn't because teaching didn't pay that much.

My husband used to give me money after getting paid, but he knew where I put it. The next day I'd find there was R10 short — and I'd find empty beer bottles.

The days he'd been drinking too much I couldn't say anything. I'd only be asking for blue eyes, you see. I'd just keep quiet and wait until early in the morning and start talking. If he hit me, I'd hit back. Really, I couldn't just watch him doing it. I'd hit back!

But my husband was sick. He had bad asthma.

After we'd been married eight years he passed away.

In some ways life was much more difficult after that. You know, I was chased out of that four-roomed house and given a two-room. They said if I couldn't get another husband in six months I had to move. I tried to explain to the superintendent that I could pay the rent, and I had two children who were growing. He said, "No", so I was chased out and I took the two-room.

I also had to do extra work. I'd buy some trousers and sell them. I got R10 or R15 more than my wage. On that wage I couldn't make it.

In other ways life was easier after he died. Because he was the one who was wasting money — drinking too much. He used to use my wages and go and get drunk.

Now it is just me and my two girls. One is eleven years and one is fifteen years. They are both staying with me in my two-roomed house. I'm going to build a spare room one of these days.

I'm still working at the same factory. There are men and women there. We do the same job, but women are not called operators. I don't know what they call me. A labourer? The man does the same job, but they call him an operator. We get almost the same wage — about R75 a week.

In another paper factory women get less than men. That's why employers like them. And also old men. There I think they are starting them with R50 or something.

They don't pay for service here. You can work for fifty years and you'll still get R75. And overtime — they force us to do it. Management says, "If you don't come in tomorrow (Saturday) then don't come in on Monday."

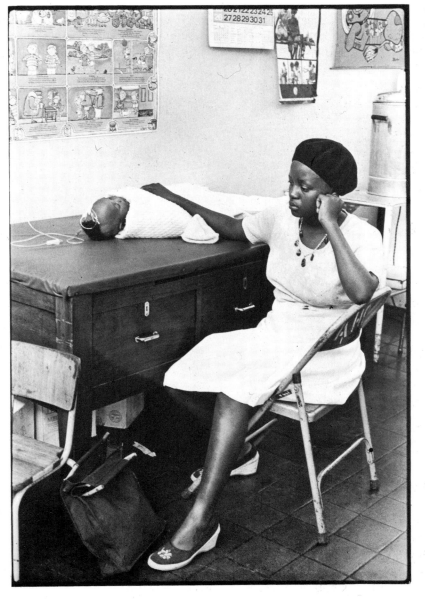

Mother with child
who is being treated
for gastro-enteritis
(Alexandra Clinic, 1980)

There were always plenty of women here — about forty women and one hundred men. Then they told us that the Industrial Council didn't want so many women in the paper industry. So they chased us, until only three girls were left.

I think it was a lie because there are plenty of women at other paper factories. I think those employers like men because they can work three shifts. Women are only allowed to work one shift.*

My life is much better than it used to be. It's not so expensive. Now that my children are older they don't get sick so often. Also, I used to spend a lot of money paying that old lady to look after them. Now they stay home after school.

My girls, I can't say that they are good girls because I don't know what they are doing when I am at work. Maybe they are only good when I come home. The younger one likes me very much. She says, "I'm not going to get married — I'll stay with you."

A lot of women don't get married these days — especially in Soweto. I've got a friend who's a social worker. She's got a baby and says she doesn't want to get married. The father wants to marry, but she won't.

I don't want my daughters to get married. If they are educated it's better that they earn a living wage. Marriage, I don't care for it. I'd like them to stay with me. They can have children and support them. They will have a better life. In Soweto marriage is no more.

I think it's caused by drinking. Men drink too much after they get married. The wife looks and thinks, "No, I can do without." Women bring the money in and men stay at home because they don't want to work. Some men are already crippled by liquor. So he's just an extra baby for the wife. He wants money for smokes and beer. She has to buy him clothes and feed him like a baby.

Women have just decided not to get married. Some are divorced — there are plenty of divorcees who won't get married again. They're tired of it. Soon there will be no more marriage. Just boyfriends and girlfriends!

(Rose Modise was interviewed in August 1983.)

* Since Rose was interviewed the law has changed. Women are now allowed to work night shift.

1

Women in the workforce

Domestic workers through the ages

Afrikana Museum

In the early part of the century it was usually men who did domestic work.

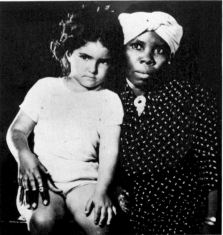

Plotz: Afrikaner Museum

Afrikana Museum

A domestic worker in the 1920s

Domestic worker and her employer's child in the 1940s

14

Today women work in many different kinds of jobs outside the home. They work as machine operators in factories, as nurses, domestic workers and farm workers. But this was not always so.

A hundred years ago most African women lived in rural areas with their men and families. They worked at ploughing the land, growing crops, cooking, caring for their children and making the things they needed in their homes.

Then in 1886 gold was discovered in the Transvaal. The mining industry and the towns around the mines began to grow very fast. The mines needed more and more men to work for them. These men became part of the migrant labour system. Their women and children were supposed to stay in the rural areas and live off the land. If a woman wanted to come to town to work, or to join her man, she had to get special permission. This permission was difficult to get. But many women broke the laws and went to the towns anyway.

Women move into the towns

At first black women came into the towns in small numbers. In 1921 only sixty-four out of every one thousand women lived in the towns.

There were few jobs for these women because most of the jobs were already taken by men. Black men even did domestic work and washing. Women had to earn money in jobs like selling, brewing beer and prostitution.

There was no proper housing for these women and their families. They lived in large slums in and around the towns.

Escaping rural poverty

It was in the 1930s that things began to change. Life in the rural areas had become more difficult for women. The Land Act of 1913 had taken much land away from the African people. Rural people were left with less than a fifth of the country's land.

This land (then called the reserves) became over-crowded and the soil became poor. It was hard to grow enough crops to feed a family.

By the 1930s very few rural people could survive by farming. They had to rely on money to buy food and other things. But there were not many paid jobs in the reserves. And the wages that the migrant men earned in town were too little to support their families in the country.

Many women realised that the only way they could save themselves and their families was to go to the towns and look for work.

Becoming domestic workers

At the same time conditions in the towns were changing. Industry was growing. White and coloured women began to work in the factories. But the factories still needed many unskilled and semi-skilled workers. Many African men began to leave domestic service for better jobs in the factories.

The African women who were coming to the towns in large numbers began to do the work that men had done. They could now get jobs as domestic workers, washerwomen and chars.

The fact that women could now get jobs encouraged them to come to the towns. In 1921 there were 12 000 African women in Johannesburg. By 1936 this number had increased five times to 60 000.

The move into the factories

African women were excluded from factory work for many years. Factory jobs were for African men, and white and coloured women. By 1946 only **one** out of every hundred women factory workers was an African woman.

During the war years many factories employed white women.

It was only in the 1960s that large numbers of African women were able to get jobs in the factories.

During the 1960s there was a great economic boom in South Africa. More and more factories were built and the cities were growing. White women began to find better jobs as secretaries, commercial workers and as supervisors in factories. Factory owners started to look around for a new source of cheap labour. African women were drawn into factory jobs in bigger numbers.

By 1963 **twenty-one** out of every hundred women factory workers were African women. By 1980 this figure had increased to **forty-three**.

New jobs

In the 1970s new service jobs became increasingly important in city life. These were jobs like office cleaning, hairdressing, cooking in fast food shops, waitressing and tea-making.

Before, many of these tasks were done by women in the home. For example, housewives or domestic workers cooked all the meals and washed all the clothes a family would need. But as more women went out to work, this began to change. Small businesses outside the home began to offer these services.

Many black women moved out of domestic service into these new jobs in the service sector. In 1973 there were 62 478 African women in these new service jobs. By 1981 this had increased to 112 024 women.

A night cleaner polishes a boardroom table. (Johannesburg, 1984)

Also in this period African women were able to get jobs as clerks and sales people. This happened on a very small scale. But for the first time black women were moving up the ladder into better-paid jobs.

Where women work

The graph on the opposite page shows where African women worked in 1970. (This is based on government figures.) Each person on the graph stands for about 20 000 women workers.

The graph shows that in 1970 the largest number of African women worked in agriculture. These are women in the bantustans, and farm workers in the white rural areas. (Chapter Four shows how women have been trapped in these areas by the government's influx control laws.)

The next biggest group of women workers was in the service sector. This group included domestic workers and women in other service jobs.

In 1970 the smallest number of African women workers were in the clerical, sales and professional jobs.

Women workers today

Today the position of women workers is similar to that of the 1970s. The government figures for 1980 are not accurate because they did not count women in the independent bantustans. But we can still learn something from the figures.

There are a few important changes. Between 1970 and 1980 the number of women increased in
— clerical and sales work (five times)
— factory work (more than two times)
— professional work (nearly two times)

So in the 1980s the majority of women workers are still in **agriculture** and **service work**. These two sectors have a lot in common — they offer the worst wages of any paying jobs. Also farm workers and domestic workers are not covered by many of the laws that protect factory workers. The conditions of these workers also make it very difficult for them to participate in trade unions. So, often these two groups of workers struggle under very bad working conditions.

In the 1980s growing numbers of women are getting jobs in factories. But as we shall see in Chapter Three these are usually the least skilled and worst paid of all factory jobs. Although factory workers are protected by some laws, these laws do not take care of women's special needs, for example the right to paid maternity leave.

The number of African women in **professional, clerical** and **sales jobs** is increasing, but it is still very small. In Chapter Two we look at some of these jobs, to see what the wages and working conditions are really like.

Employment of African women workers. (1970)

Agricultural workers = 44%	
Service workers = 37%	
Unclassifiable workers = 11%	
Industrial workers = 4%	
Professional workers = 3%	
Clerical and sales workers = 1%	

The first line of this chart shows what percentage
of African women workers in 1970 were doing agricultural work.
The chart shows clearly that at that time most women workers
did service (including domestic work) and agricultural jobs.

Anna Moloi cleans
nineteen passageways
every day.
(Braamfontein, 1980)

Nomvula

In the interview that follows, Nomvula talks about her work as a cleaner. Many of the problems she has are common among the women who work in service jobs. She also talks about her problems as a working mother and wife. Nomvula, like so many women in the 1980s, is fighting for a better life with the help of her trade union.

I've been doing night work for about twenty years, if I'm not mistaken.

Now I'm cleaning an office building. I start work at six o'clock at night and work through till three o'clock or half past three. There are sixty of us in the different office buildings. In my building we are four.

That work is not good for a woman. When we knock off it is dangerous to go in the street. There are so many tsotsis. And there's no transport. So we have to try and sleep till morning, and there's nowhere to sleep. In the daytime it's also hard to sleep because sometimes it's hot, and there's a lot of noise in the location.

The people leave those offices very dirty. There's paper everywhere, and sometimes even cigarettes on the floor. It's dirty, that is why we work the whole night. And we've got to clean the toilets as well. Each one of us has a whole floor to do, and that floor is big.

On my floor I've got five toilets and two kitchens. And those toilets are so huge inside, you could put your bed and wardrobe there and make it a room.

Every night I clean in the same way. You must start with emptying the dustbins and ashtrays. Then you dust — and you must dust the pictures on the walls (*laughs*), clean them nicely. After that you hoover the carpets with the machine. And there's a huge big buffing machine for the floors. On Fridays you must put polish in the toilets, and on the stair-case and furniture. Friday is too much work.

Those machines are so heavy. Sometimes you have terrible backache and your hands are tired. They're machines for men really.

When you've finished your work you go downstairs to wash the dusting rags and clean the machines. Once we've finished we wash ourselves and we sleep there until half past five.

We sleep in our changing rooms. The place is sometimes very cold. There's no carpet on the floor — only tiles. You just take cardboard boxes and sleep on the floor. Sometimes you sit in the chair and you sleep sitting like this, because it's cold on the floor. Or you turn on the hot plate to warm the room.

After sleeping, we wash ourselves again and we walk to the station. It's still dangerous then, but if we sleep till half past seven we reach Soweto at nine o'clock, and that's too late. People with children have to be there to prepare food for them and help them get ready for school. In winter you know you must come and make sure the children have got warm jerseys and all that. I am luckier because my mother does that job for me. I just have to go home and sleep.

So we get home at seven o'clock or half past seven. Then I sleep at about half past eight. At midday I wake up because I must make the fire, and cook. Then I must wash myself and prepare to catch a two o'clock bus which takes me to the station. The station is too far, and the trains are few at that time of day. If I miss my bus, I am late at work.

I used to live with my mother in Meadowlands. It was a two-roomed house and I've got my own four children and my brother's children as well. We were nine altogether. And the toilet is inside. If that toilet is blocked, you've got to stay outside.

The house was too small. We were sleeping from the kitchen to the dining room. It was not comfortable for us, sleeping on the floor.

Now it's better because we've got our place — my husband and I. It's a backyard room. We pay R60 a month. It's too much for only a one-roomed house. You can just fit in your bed and your wardrobe.

My children stay at my mother's. I try to go every weekend to see my children and take them some food. I miss them, but I've got no choice because they can't sleep there alone at night. You see, my husband is also working at night. He's a security guard in the same company as me.

My husband gets home at about eight in the morning because he knocks off at six. When he comes he sleeps — because he's got no children to wash. He just sleeps. And he sometimes wakes up at one o'clock and I give him food.

He doesn't help at home. No! (*laughs*). Because you know they say that a husband is a big man. He shouldn't do anything at home — the woman must work. We both work at night, but he can't help me with anything. When he's at home he must have a rest, and I must cook for him.

He thinks if his friends find him sweeping they're going to say he's stupid. So he can't do anything. He just sits there with the paper.

On the weekends there's lots to do at home — wash your washing and iron it. Clean the house, cook for your husband, go to church. And you sleep at night.

This job makes me sick. You've got sore eyes and you've got headaches all the time because you don't sleep full hours.

Some women take snuff to keep themselves awake at work. We're taking tablets — like Disprin and Compral — so that we don't sleep. Because you can't work when you are feeling sleepy.

The tablets aren't healthy, but what can we do because we've got headaches and sore feet from standing all night, and backache from scrubbing — going up and down like that. And you've got tension, you feel dizzy, you don't know how you are. That's why you take tablets.

Sometimes we just feel like leaving. But we've got no choice. If we could get easier jobs, we'd do it. But there's no work in South Africa. We must pay rent, we must feed our children. That's why we do night shift!

I've tried to look for other work but it's not easy. You go there to the Polly (*Polly Street labour office*) and you can stay there for the whole day. Sometimes you find someone who wants a 'girl' but when you get there you find the jobs are not suitable, and they don't pay enough.

Now they're paying us R315 — and they're pulling for tax and all that. And they don't pay for transport. My husband gets R348 — and the securities don't do such hard work because they sit on their chairs the whole night. But that job is dangerous. If someone comes and breaks the doors, they must fight for their lives.

I joined the union in 1981 and I became a shop

8.30 a.m. Night nurse on her way home (Soweto, 1982)

steward in 1983. I joined because our bosses didn't pay. And if you made a small mistake they would kick you out of the job.

Also, we didn't have any maternity rights. If you were going to have a child, they'd book you off — discharge you.

These are all the reasons why we joined the union. And the union has helped us.

We had negotiations with management. They're so hard. They don't want to give us money. They've got their lawyers there. They just gave us all R33 on top of our wages.

Our bosses, you know, when I look at them I see they are in South Africa for money. They don't care about us. They care about their jobs and money. They should provide transport for us at night, but they can't because they are so greedy about money.

We tried to get a night shift allowance — that is extra money for night workers. But they didn't agree with that. They said if they give us a night shift allowance then all the workers will want to work at night and they'll have no people to work in the day. It's not true, it's just a trick. Because, you know, if you're a boss you can't just give your money away.

But we were so happy because our union tries. They've helped us to get maternity rights. They've made them buy tea for us to drink at work. They've made them to buy hot plates and kettles. Before the union was in, there was no table, no chairs, no changing rooms. Now we've got all these things.

We asked management about transport. They said they're not sure, they said they were going to try. But I think they'll run away about transport because since the union is in they're using a lot of money.

It's hard for us night workers to go to union meetings. But we go because we enjoy it, and it helps us. But it's hard because we don't sleep. Especially on a Saturday when we've got a shop stewards council meeting. We have to stay at work and go to the meeting at half past seven.

But we enjoy the meetings, because this union helps us with many things — even if a person's dismissed.

Once we had a superintendent at our place. When she heard that I was a unionist and a shop steward she dismissed me. When I talked to them in the office they said they wouldn't discharge me. But they wanted me to work in another building.

When I thought about it, I thought that they wanted to get me out because they thought I would make the other workers interested in the union. So I didn't agree to move. But I did ask for a good reason why the superintendent didn't want me there. They had a big surprise.

I went to my union and told them the story. And they made a meeting with my boss, and he agreed that I should have my job back. When the superintendent heard that I was back, she decided to go. She was so cross, I thought she was going to kill me.

That woman was terrible you know. She used to fight with the people. On pay day we were supposed to get our cheques at night — but she used to give them out at ten o'clock in the morning. So we night workers had to wait long after work.

Before she gave you the money she would shout at you, "Jy werk niks but jy kry baie tjeld." (*laughs*). So every month-end it's a song and dance. And she used to dismiss people for nothing. She used to say,

Office cleaner and security guard (Johannesburg, 1984)

"I hate a black person because a black person has killed my father." Rude words like that.

So when she learnt that I was in the union she realised that all this was going to stop. She knew she'd be out, that's why she wanted me out.

You know, we like our union. It makes us brave. Now we can talk to them. Before they could just dismiss you without any reason. If the induna doesn't like you − or if he wants love with you, and you don't want it − he would just go to the superintendent and tell her that you don't work properly. And the superintendent wouldn't come to you and ask you why − she would just chase you out.

Now that the union is here we have a dismissal procedure. I have to take it step by step − starting with the superintendent. And if we're not settled, I must take it to the management. They don't like it. They just want to be able to say, "Gaan uit jong, gaan uit," and skop you uit. But now they can't do all those things.

My husband also belongs to the union, but he's not a shop steward. (laughs). You know he's got a shop steward in his building but he prefers to come to me with his problems. So he likes it that I'm a shop steward. He doesn't want to be a shop steward. He's afraid to talk with people. But he likes the union very much. He sees that the union is working.

The position of women workers is too heavy, with many things.

The first thing: say you are a woman and you are looking for a job. When you reach a factory, you find the induna there and you ask him. If you like the job the induna will tell you that you must sleep with him before you get that job.

And you've got no choice. You want to work and your children are starving in Soweto. So, some women sleep with those men. Some women sleep with the bosses because they want more money, or easier work. They do it because they want to live, not because they're mad or what.

Then, when you are working there, a new woman comes and the induna wants to sleep with her. And you, you're nothing inside now. And your husband may leave you because you've got another man's baby − and you've only slept with that man because you wanted the job.

It's sick, all that.

(Nomvula was interviewed in August 1984.)

Women's work

2

What makes women's work so very different from the work that men do?

Many women workers have completely different jobs from men. For example, more than one third of all black women workers are service workers. Only a very small proportion of male workers are in service work.

Serving and caring

In our society service work, or servicing other people, is seen as women's work. At home women are always expected to serve and care for their families. Few men will help with this kind of work.

Why is this "women's work"?

At work women also find themselves in jobs that involve serving and caring for other people. These are jobs like domestic work, office cleaning and laundry work.

When we look outside the service sector itself, we also find many women in service and caring kinds of jobs. Teachers are educating children, nurses are caring for sick people, clerical workers are servicing managers and administrators in the office.

Even women factory workers are in 'home-like' sorts of jobs. Most women factory workers are making food and clothing.

If we add up all the women in these 'home-like' jobs they account for more than half of all black women workers.

Low value and low pay

But there is another important feature of women's jobs. Not only are they 'home-like', but they are also badly paid and offer poor working conditions.

It seems that society does not value the 'home-like' jobs – even though serving and caring is important work. At home this work is unpaid and taken for granted. At work it is seen as unskilled and unimportant.

Men do not want to do this kind of work because of its low value and poor working conditions. So it remains 'women's work'.

The low value of women's jobs is not only a South African problem. All around the world women find themselves in serving and caring jobs. For example, in Britain three out of four women workers are in service jobs. Their jobs are also badly paid and undervalued.

In this chapter we discuss domestic work, nursing and teaching to show the low wages and poor conditions which women workers face. In Chapter Three we look at the similar problems of women factory workers who work in 'women's industries'.

Domestic work

Domestic work fits the description of 'women's work' in every way. Domestic workers spend their days and nights serving others. They are also among the worst-paid and least-protected workers in this country.

No minimum wage

There is no legal minimum wage for domestic workers. Wages are decided by the employer – and they vary a lot. In 1981 the average wage for domestic workers was R32 a month. (If the cost of food and housing are included it increases to R59.)

SADWA (the South African Domestic Workers Association) is calling for a minimum wage of R165 a month for a skilled, full-time, live-in domestic worker. This is very much less than most legally set minimum wages. For example, the minimum wage for a labourer in the baking industry is R239,98 a month.

Domestic worker at opening of art exhibition (Johannesburg, 1984)

I did a long apprenticeship for my job. I cooked from when I was a little girl.
I did my first dinner at home when I was eight years old. My mother taught me everything.
It should be seen as an apprenticeship. Cooking is a skilled job.

Barbara, a British trade unionist who works in a nursery as a cook.

At a shopping centre (Southdale, Johannesburg, 1981)

No legal rights

Domestic work is excluded from the Basic Conditions of Employment Act. This law lays down minimum working conditions like hours of work, sick leave and holidays. So domestic workers have no legal rights to paid holidays or a fixed working day.

Domestic workers are also not covered by the Unemployment Insurance Fund, which gives unemployment, sickness and maternity benefits. These women workers are completely at their employers' mercy and goodwill.

Margaret Nhlapo of SADWA says: Domestic workers each have different problems, because they work for different employers — and people are different. One thing in common is low wages.

For example, somebody came last week to complain — she is earning R30 a month, and she has been working for those people for twenty-two years! What can you do with R30 today? It's a bag of mealies — you work for a whole month for a bag of mealies and nothing extra.

People in the white suburbs are really exploiting domestic workers to such an extent. But you also find it in Soweto. People go out to the farms and they get these very young girls of about twelve to fourteen years, and pay them R20 to R40 a month. These children are suffering just like their mothers are doing in the suburbs.

The worst thing that employers do is kick out their domestic workers when they are old and tired.

A friend of mine worked for this family — almost her whole life. She worked while the children grew up and the mother died. When the father was an old man he became ill. She was a nursemaid to him. She was the only one who looked after him. She gave him his medicine, and watched over him at night.

Okay, so the old man dies. She phones the daughters. She's undressed the old man and she's taken a nice sheet to put it over him, and phoned the doctor.

The children came and the undertaker came and took care of the body. The children called her and asked her to tidy up the flat. She washed the sheets and so on, and she went to her room.

She stayed in that room for three weeks. The children never came to see her, to see if she had something to eat, or anything. Neither of those two children thought of her. The old man had not left her anything — and they didn't give her a cent. They sold his carpets, furniture and everything. They just gave her all the old rubbish. They didn't give a damn.

Oppressive relationships

The relationship that exists between domestic workers and their employers is often very oppressive. It is a one to one relationship which is not controlled by any law of contract. Many employers treat their domestic workers like children who have to be disciplined, rather than responsible adults.

Stephanie: I once worked for a very unkind woman. She'd like to come and show you when you hadn't cleaned well. And the food — I can't speak about the food. Any cupboard she used to lock. Sometimes she forgot the keys and left them in the lock when she went to work. Then she'd phone home and say, "Oh Stephanie, please call one of my children and tell them to hide the keys away." I'd just look and say, 'hayi'.

Rose: I found domestic work in Brixton. The madam used to say, "Rose, you mustn't iron your clothes here. Here's your plate, here's your cup — you mustn't use my crockery."

I don't like those kinds of people. It's as if I'm dirty, or she's going to become black.

You don't want me to sit on your chair, but I work in your house. I give you food, like that, with my own hands, but you don't want me to use your things.

Elsie: Domestic work is too much for me. The employer wants you to come early, but when it's time for you to knock off, he or she forgets that you must be early at home also. You can't ask your employer, "Why are you late?" You are 'the girl' for the employer.

I was a factory worker for ten years. In the factories when it's four o'clock knock off, it's four o'clock. If it's overtime, six o'clock in the morning and six o'clock 'shayile'. If that bell rings, everybody must stop what they are doing.

I think when you work as a domestic, it's a battle with the madam in her house. She can talk rude to you because you're late. But you can't say, "No madam, don't be rude to me."

Jobs for rural women

Because domestic work is known to be low-paid and unpleasant, it is mostly done by women who have no other skills or job opportunities.

During the last twenty years the number of live-in domestic workers has dropped. It seems that more and more domestic workers are going into part-time or charring work — or other kinds of jobs. This way they can earn more and have greater freedom.

Over the years it has been rural women, desperately in need of wages and housing, who have gone into domestic service. Even though the 'homes' provided are mostly small rooms in lonely backyards, they are prized by rural women. Accommodation is one of the reasons why 'illegal' workers are attracted to domestic work. But with the tightening up of influx control, and the recession squeezing white households, it has become harder and harder for these women to get jobs.

Stephanie: Hayi, two years in Germiston and I was working for R40 only.

I've got children there at home. It's just me and my brother who supports them. They need a lot of money. Things are very bad.

I used to try and save up my salary and send them R40 every second month. It's too heavy. There's no rain on the farm. They did plough. No rain. They need money. They have to buy mealie meal at the shops. School fees are going up. Money.

I'm looking for some other job. I've been looking for eight weeks and it's hard. I've looked everywhere. I've asked all my friends. I've knocked on doors. But even if the madam did need someone she wouldn't say, because nowadays you can't trust a person walking off the street.

My pass is not right. It causes a big problem. Hayi, I'll just see . . . Maybe I'll be lucky.

So the number of women who are willing and legally able to do full-time domestic work is decreasing. The nature of domestic service in South Africa may be slowly changing.

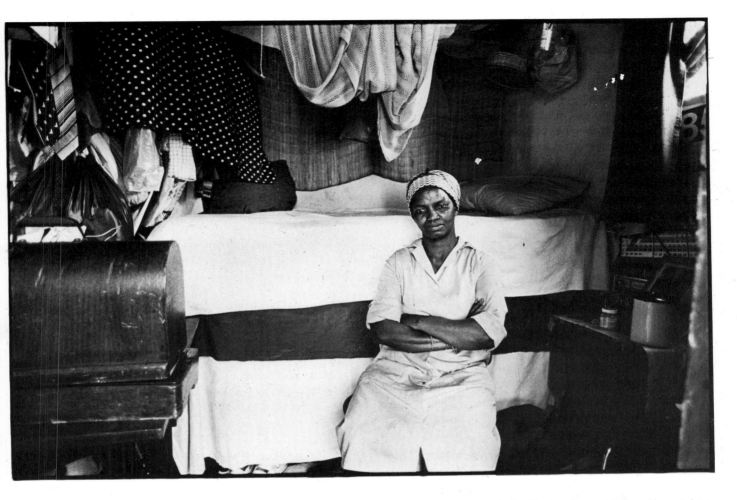

Julia Mwkwebane, domestic worker,
in her backyard room (Johannesburg, 1985)

Domestic workers worry a lot.
Say for instance you are looking after somebody's children —
but you don't even know what your own children are doing.
You will worry about whether they have slept, and if they are happy.

Margaret Nhlapo. SADWA.

Elizabeth Tschayinca

Elizabeth Tshayinca and Elsie Mbatha

Elizabeth Tshayinca and her daughter Elsie Mbatha have both worked as domestic workers for many years. Elsie has also worked in a factory and now plans to earn her living as a hawker.

Elizabeth works for one employer and commutes daily between Soweto and Johannesburg. Elsie works part-time for a number of employers.

In this interview they discuss the problems they have had as domestic workers. Elsie explains why she prefers to be a hawker rather than a domestic worker or factory worker. They also discuss the advantages and disadvantages of live-in and charring work.

Elizabeth: Oh, I've been doing domestic work for more than fifty years. Count the years from eleven to sixty-six: it's fifty-five years. I was eleven years old when I started work for this family and I used to look after the little girl – earning a pound a month. That's how I started.

Before, I was a live-in domestic. I did that for a long time, until I had five or six children. My mother looked after the children.

It's worse when you live in. No rest, day and night. If they go out at night they want you to come and sit with their children. No pay for that, you see.

Elsie: Domestic work! You earn peanuts – even when you do a part-time job.

Elizabeth: You know what, you can work part-time and earn more. But you work hard. You can't say yesterday I scrubbed cupboards, today I'm not scrubbing cupboards. I must scrub cupboards today because I'm doing this job only for that day. That means you've always got to have that full strength to work every day.

Elsie: When you do a part-time job maybe you come once or twice a week, or once or twice a month. That job will be a whole month's job. You must do it in one day. You do the fridge, you do the stove, do the windows – and you must finish it in one day. Ayi khona! I'm not a machine.

The employer says you've got one hour for lunch. But there's no hour. Instead of sitting down and eating your food, you're rushing to finish this job. You don't even chew nicely – you're just rushing to swallow because you're watching the time.

You get up early, you go to work early – but you come home late. That's what makes people unhappy about domestic work. It's slavery.

I cook for my husband. He's tired from work, lifting up heavy boxes and iron. Sometimes we come in at the same time. He wants his tea. He'll sit down with the paper. You'll be a 'girl' again in the house. He is the boss reading the paper. And that makes you fed up. By the time you go to sleep you're tired.

You've had no time to sit down and talk to him, or listen to the radio, or watch TV. You must wash up and go to bed. That's when you relax.

I've been selling fruit and veggies at the station in Soweto. I make from R10 to R40 a day. But I've stopped because I'm waiting for a licence. The inspectors worry us and we get caught. It's hard to get a licence. They make you dance in their offices for a long time before they give you one.

If I can get this licence I'll stop working because I can see where there's money. Any time, any day, I'll stop working. Maybe for safety's sake I can stay with one employer for my pass — in case the superintendent wants me to produce my pass. He can see that it is registered.

Factory work? No, I won't go back there. I want my own business. I want to sit down and forget about other people's jobs. Do my own. That's why I'm waiting for this licence. As soon as it comes, oh, I'll be saying Happy Christmas! S'true.

Once I lived in, for Jewish people in Orange Grove. They had big girls, but they were so rude. Screaming at you, making themselves 'madams' in the house. Telling you, "You didn't press my pants nicely. My blouse has got a creased collar." And you must fix it up. Not talking nicely — screaming at you, pulling faces, bringing their big eyes out. And if you shout back the mother comes and says, "Look here, you must listen to the little madams because I'm paying you."

Another thing — you've also got to remember the employer's mother. The mother comes to show you even though she doesn't pay you: "There's a cobweb in the corner, please try and get it off, I can't stand it." And then she comes picking up a paper from the passage and says to you, "Here's your present." You must browse around and see if there are some more. And that's annoying also.

If you are not satisfied it's best to keep quiet. If you can't stand it, say goodbye nicely; don't be cross. Give a big smile.

Elizabeth: You know, I've come across many things of the same kind. But I don't worry about them. No, I don't worry about them. No, I don't exchange words — unless they swear. I just keep quiet and look at them. They don't know what I'm thinking inside. The next thing it's the end of the month. I get my wages and I go. I'll just forget them.

Elsie: You don't make her say sorry. Just say, "No, I'm going to build a house in the homelands" or "my husband doesn't want me to work any more." These are the reasons we give our employers.

Then, when the employer gets a new 'girl' she'll blacklist you. She'll say, "This one used to steal from my freezer. You know, I had a leg of lamb. The next thing it's gone."

If you've got long service with your employer they'll always tell stories and make trouble so that you must leave. And when you leave, you don't get your full money. They rob you of your wages, rob you of your notice pay and then from there, rob you of your service pay.

Elizabeth: I'd like to tell you this. Our children don't want to do domestic work. That's why I think people have invented these new machines for cleaning and washing. In places like England there's nobody to do housework, like we do here.

Elsie: In the future Gogo, I don't think there'll be such a thing as domestic work.

Elizabeth: Oh, there'll still be, because not everybody has got the money to pay for their children to be educated. Unless of course there's free education. Even now, people who have the money don't send their children to school.

Elsie: Especially girls.

Elizabeth: Especially girls, you see. It's nonsense not to send girls to school. Because, say now a girl gets married and that marriage breaks. If she's been to school, she'll have something that keeps her going. She can work for herself. If she's not educated she'll end up like me. Scrubbing somebody's floors.

Elsie Mbatha

Elsie: Climbing on the windows like me. (*laughter*)

Elizabeth: Now I look around at all those people who started work after me. They're not working any more, they're sitting down. They're getting their pensions from where they used to work. People who were clever, who were the school teachers and the nurses and all those things, ja man.

You're asking me about retirement? If I stop work, I stop wages. I have to keep on working until I don't know when, because this domestic work has got no pension.

I haven't got money saved. Very little. Are you going to give me some? I've worked for some people for over twenty years. What do I get? Nothing.

But I can say I've come across some very good people. No nonsense. You know why, because they ask me favours and I'll do things for them. No argument. The word behind everything is 'please'. You see?

(Elizabeth and Elsie were interviewed in September 1984.)

Other kinds of service work

Other workers in the service sector are better off than domestic workers. These are women in jobs like office cleaning, laundry work and tea-making. These service workers at least have the protection of the laws which set down minimum wages and working conditions.

But these service workers still experience many of the problems of 'women's work'. Their jobs, like Nomvula's which she describes on pages 21/26, are often underpaid, hard and tiring. The minimum wage for cleaners, for example, is R38 a week. Many service jobs have to be done at night, and night work causes health and social problems.

Other kinds of service work ►

Clerical work –
another form of serving

Joan Sinqoto, private secretary

Taking notes at a meeting

Miriam Molobve, receptionist

It's peace when there's no one in the office. Then I try to rush, rush —
do everything, so that when they come I'll be ready for them.
Somebody will say 'type this', someone will say 'please make a phone call for me'.

Liza Makalela. Trade union office administrator.

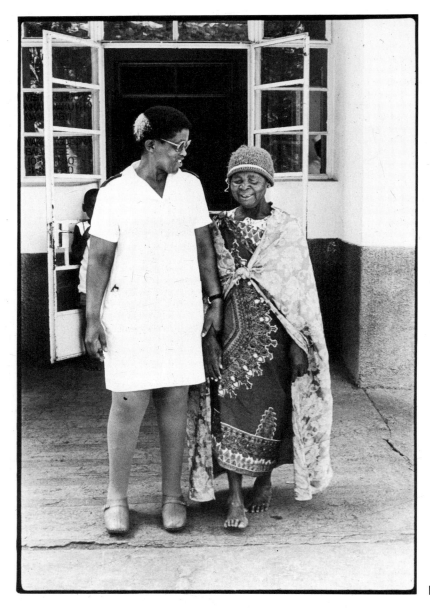

Nurse with a blind patient (Elim Hospital, 1980)

'Professional' women

Women have always tried to escape from the drudgery and poor conditions of service work into professional and clerical jobs. After the Second World War white women moved into these jobs. In the 1970s and 1980s it became easier for black women to get professional and clerical jobs.

Nurses and teachers

The most common kinds of professional jobs for women are nursing and teaching. Although these jobs are valued by many communities, they lack the status and high salaries of other professions. Of all the professions, nursing and teaching are the most like 'women's work', so these are the jobs which are easiest for women to get.

In 1981 nine out of every ten black professional women were nurses or teachers. In the same year six out of every ten white women were nurses or teachers. In other words, white women find it easier to get jobs in the better-paid professions than black women do. The better-paid, higher status jobs are the ones done by scientific researchers, doctors, architects, graphic artists, etc.

Disadvantages

Even within the professions of nursing and teaching black women are at a disadvantage. The majority of these women are under-qualified. They are also in the lowest grades of work, and they earn low wages.

For example, one of every ten black teachers has no professional training, and has gone no further in school than Standard Eight. Most of these untrained teachers are women. Although they are not qualified, the work they do is skilled and demanding. But because they lack qualifications their status and pay is low.

Two out of every three black nurses are students or nursing assistants. They do all the most menial jobs in the hospital. Some of their work is very similar to ordinary domestic work — making beds, making tea, washing and cleaning.

Low wages, low status

A black woman who has passed Standard Seven and who starts teaching without a teacher's diploma earns only R112 a month. This is lower than the wage earned by many factory workers.

Also, women teachers are found teaching the lower grades. Most women teachers are in primary schools, and most men in secondary schools. Very few women get promoted to principal in secondary schools — almost all high school principals are men.

Of course, women can and do make it into well-paid high status professional jobs, but such women are relatively few. The majority of black professional women are in jobs that have few advantages over domestic and factory work. The stories of Catherine and Maureen, on the following pages, describe some of the problems of black professional women.

Dolly Moloko, attorney at the Centre for Applied Legal Studies
(University of Witwatersrand, 1985)

Miriam Mazibuko, social worker,
talks to a client.
(Johannesburg, 1985)

Petunia Maboe and Natie Rule,
actresses in the play 'Call me woman'
(Market Theatre, Johannesburg, 1979)

Catherine and her students (Transkei, 1984)

Catherine

Catherine teaches at a school in Transkei.

I started being a class teacher in 1980. Since I started, I've taught all subjects. Even now.

Really, the problem I meet is a matter of the subjects which were difficult for me at school. The worst one was maths. Now I teach maths to Standard Three and Four.

We all take two classes at once in this school. It's very difficult because the syllabuses are not the same. Some of the children cannot understand Xhosa or seSotho. So the teacher has to talk two languages. At the end of every day you feel lousy. Every day, every day — tired.

Catherine and her fellow teachers

I've been interested in teaching ever since I was a schoolgirl. I talked to my parents about it and they agreed. So I went to training school. The main thing I was interested in was keeping up my nation.

I saw it was difficult when I was still young — looking at the other teachers — it's really difficult to teach, to turn someone's mind to become something.

If I had the means I'd like to do typing. But I have no means to go back to school. There is no one to help my parents since my sisters are married, so I am the one who is supporting them. I buy groceries and clothes for my parents and the five children. I earn R337.

(Catherine was interviewed in August 1984.)

Maureen with a patient in the old age home

Maureen Sithole

In 1982 Maureen Sithole was an unregistered nursing assistant working in an old age home in Johannesburg. She left her previous job at a factory because she wanted to learn the skill of caring for people.

I work nights, night shift only. We start at 5.30 p.m. and work until 6.30 in the morning. I leave home at 3.30 p.m. I go by bus. The first thing we do is make sure that the ward is tidy. Then you look at your patients to see how they are. Maybe you find bruises or the patient has changed. Then you make tea, feed them — those who can't feed themselves. After tea you go to the kitchen. We wash up and tidy the place. Then back to the wards.

Now we do two-hourly turning, three times a night. You turn them and you rub that other side.

Four o'clock and you wake them up and wash them. Then tidy up the beds. Put on clean linen. That's all for the night.

The work is all right, there is nothing wrong with it. And the old ladies are all right — they give us no trouble. With my job I am satisfied. This is a thing I want to do. But I am not satisfied with the salary. I earn R100 a month. We even have to buy our own uniforms with that R100.

I have liked nursing from childhood, to be of help to the society. Not for my own benefit, not for gain — I mean to have that knowledge of helping the sick. I used to feel pity for a person who can't do anything for herself.

It takes me a long time to get home from work. I reach home at about 8.30 a.m. or quarter to nine. When I get home, the first thing I do is make myself a cup of tea. Then if my daughter is not home I

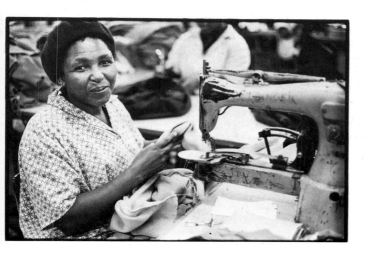

In the factory I was size 40."

"Now I am size 36."

must see about the house, tidy up, make the bed. I must clean. After that make some breakfast.

Then I sleep for a few hours. Two hours or three. Sometimes twelve to two. Sometimes eleven to two. But I don't sleep longer than that — that's for sure. On the weekends it is worse. I don't sleep at all on weekends. We have got neighbours this side and that side and they are drinking. They are so noisy. They open their grams and you can't sleep at all when there is noise.

We work seven days on and three days off — seven days you must work it. I am tired at the end of seven days, but I do manage. Sometimes you feel funny. Sometimes you feel fresh. There are days when you feel sleepy during the night. You must feel drowsy, like it or not.

It does affect me. There are days when I feel very, very tired. As if I am not well. I've got thinner from lack of sleep. At the factory I was size forty. Now I am a size thirty-six.

I used to work in a factory — I was a machinist there. I left that job because I wanted to be a nurse. I saw this advertisement in the newspaper. They said they would train a person to be a nurse aide. Now I am here and I find they don't train us formally. I want a nurse aide certificate, but I can't get it here. Although at this place I do all the work that a nurse aide would do. It's just that this place is not registered, so we can't get our certificates from here.

Now I am doing a separate course to get my nurse aide certificate. I have to go to lectures in the day — twice a week. This means that I pay extra. It also means that there are two days in the week when I don't get any sleep at all.

(Maureen Sithole was interviewed in April 1982.)

3

In the factories

Women who work in the factories have a better deal than most service workers. Factory workers are covered by laws which lay down minimum wages and working conditions. Although these minimums are low, they do give some protection.

Also, factory workers have trade unions to help them in their struggle for better wages and working conditions. And yet black women factory workers still face many problems.

As we saw in Chapter One, African women were the last group of workers to move into factory work. The jobs they got were the lowest-paid and the least skilled.

One trade unionist described who did what jobs in the clothing industry in 1952. He said that the head cutters and designers were skilled men and women from Europe. Afrikaans men and women were also beginning to move into these top jobs.

The least skilled work was operative or semi-skilled work. All of this work was done by women. The more experienced white and coloured women sewed the better clothes and worked with finer cloth. The cheapest clothes — like khaki trousers and overalls — were made by coloured, Indian and African women.

From this description we can see that black women were at the bottom of the employment ladder.

Changing jobs

It was in the 1960s that African women started to move into factory work in greater numbers than before. This was also a time when there were big changes in factory work.

In the 1960s factory owners bought new machinery to make their factories more profitable. This machinery took the place of many skilled workers. Now factories started using semi-skilled workers to operate the machines. It was these semi-skilled jobs which were offered to African women.

One can see these changes clearly by looking at the textile industry.

Up until the 1960s there were many skilled weavers in the textile industry. These weavers had to train for a long time before they could work the looms. During the 1960s the factory owners bought semi-automatic weaving machines. The new machines did not need so much skilled attention. For example, they could stop by themselves if the thread was torn.

These new machines could be operated by workers with very little training. The employers offered these new semi-skilled jobs to African women. Over time the women took the place of the more skilled African men. By the early 1970s most weavers were semi-skilled African women.

Because the semi-skilled workers needed less training than skilled workers, employers paid them lower wages. For example, a survey in 1964 showed that the average wage for semi-skilled workers in Johannesburg was R35,68 a month. In the same year the average wage for skilled workers in Johannesburg was R65,54 a month.

A woman operator minds a textile machine. (Johannesburg, 1981)

Filling the drying rack

The 'women's industries'

Today most black women factory workers are still stuck in these lower-paid semi-skilled jobs. Black women factory workers are also trapped in particular industries. These are the 'home-like' industries — food, clothing, textile and leather.

The 'home-like' industries are known for their low wages and poor working conditions. And all around the world it is women who work in them. One British writer describes these industries as 'female employment ghettos'.

South African government surveys show the lower wages paid in the 'women's industries'. In 1982 the average monthly wage for factory workers was R360 a month. Workers in the 'women's industries' earned less than this. For example, the average monthly wages for clothing and food workers were R154 and R242 a month. Workers in the mainly male metal industry earned an average of R387 a month.

Women find themselves in these 'home-like' industries because society defines this work as 'women's work'. Making clothes and food seems like the work that women do at home.

As one official of the Clothing Industrial Council said, "... by natural upbringing women are more geared to operating sewing machines and making clothes and so on..."

Many people think this way. But very few women workers learn to use sewing machines at home; they learn on the job. In the earlier description of the clothing industry we saw that all the important and creative jobs were done by men. People didn't think it was natural for women to be good at these jobs — which were more interesting and better paid.

In fact most 'women's' jobs are nothing like the work women do at home. Which housewife packs eggs or marks pockets all day long? These industries are women's industries simply because they employ women — and they pay lower wages than 'male' industries.

Women and men

Even when black women and men work in the same industries, women are often put into lower-paying grades of work. One trade union official says:

"Putting women into 'light industrial work' and men into 'heavy industrial work' was grounds for Smith and Nephew to pay women much less than men. The labels themselves became justifications for lower pay.

But why should it be women who do these jobs? It is thought that women have special qualities. Their 'nimble fingers' for example, which apparently enable them to sort rotting rags into colour bins in the textile industry. Or their 'creativity' which enables them to stick flower transfers on to enamel pots day in and day out."

When women and men do the same job there is still a pay gap in many cases. Up until 1981 the law allowed

Gallo agrees to equal pay for women

By STEVEN FRIEDMAN
Labour Correspondent

THE Commercial, Catering, and Allied Workers' Union (Ccawusa) has signed an agreement with Gallo (Africa) which will ensure that women doing the same work as men receive the same pay.

The union also described wage increases negotiated between it and employers as "perhaps the best this year".

Ccawusa also said yesterday it had reached an agreement with wholesalers Makro which would increase pay for all workers at three of the company's outlets by R50 a month.

At Gallo, a Ccawusa spokesman said an agreement signed yesterday would raise the pay of workers earning R100 a week or less by R8,25 a week. Those earning between R100 and R150 would receive an R11-a-week rise and those earning above R150 would get R13,50 extra.

He said the agreement was valid for six months. The two sides would negotiate a further increase in mid-year.

The spokesman said pay discrimination between men and women workers would now be eliminated.

Before the agreement, the minimum for women had been R2 a week lower than that for men, and women earning the minimum would therefore receive a R10,50 a week increase, he said.

A company spokesman, Mr Malcolm James, confirmed the agreement and said about 300 workers were covered by it.

He added that the difference between men and women's pay had, in the past, been much greater than R2 a week, but the company had been moving towards pay equality between the sexes for some time.

"The agreement therefore completes this process, which was initiated by the company", Mr James said. He added that about 5% of the company's women workers were doing the same jobs as men.

At Makro, the R50 increase will apply for the whole of next year and is the result of a verbal agreement between the company and the union. A formal wage agreement is due to be signed soon.

The increase covers the company's outlets at Pretoria, Amalgam (Industria) and Germiston. It is understood that minimum wages will rise by about 22%.

A company spokesman has confirmed the agreement.

women workers to earn 20% less than men who did the same job. Now the law says that the minimum wage rates for women and men must be the same. But the law does not prevent employers from paying women the minimum wage and paying men a higher wage. The newspaper article on this page shows the success of one trade union in fighting this pay gap in one workplace.

Operating a plastic welding machine
(Olifantsfontein, 1984)

Workers in a clothing factory
(Johannesburg, 1984)

A leather worker uses her finger to glue strips of material. (Johannesburg, 1984)

Hand sewing in a Johannesburg knitwear factory (1981)

Drying the ink on a folder in a Johannesburg silkscreen factory (1984)

No maternity rights

A major problem for women workers is the question of maternity rights.

There is no law that protects a pregnant women from losing her job. Many women lose their jobs when they become pregnant. As one factory worker says, "When management sees you are pregnant, you just get fired on that day."

This problem causes women to take unpleasant and unsafe contraception like the Depo Provera injection. This kind of contraception is often the only kind offered at management-run clinics.

Fear of losing their jobs even causes some women to try and hide their pregnancies. This can be dangerous for the mother and baby. For example, one woman strapped herself down so tightly that she miscarried when she was eight and a half months pregnant.

Also, there are no proper maternity benefits for pregnant women. Women workers who become pregnant have to rely on Unemployment Insurance Fund (UIF) benefits. These provide a maximum of 45% of the worker's wage for six months (four months before, and two months after the birth of the baby). The benefits are usually not enough for women to live on — especially if they are single women.

There is no law which says a factory must give a woman worker her job back after her baby is born. So for factory workers pregnancy very often means retrenchment.

Health problems

There are many hazards which threaten the health of women factory workers. Pregnant women who work in certain jobs may damage their unborn babies or even miscarry.

When a pregnant woman has to lift heavy weights she may suffer a miscarriage. Managers often don't care about the work they give pregnant workers. The manager of one Johannesburg dry-cleaner used to call the heavy steam-pressing machine 'the abortion machine'. This was because so many pregnant women had miscarriages whilst working on this machine.

Mother of 3 cut in half by machine

21/6/84

POTCHEFSTROOM. — A mother of three was sliced in half last week in a Potchefstroom factory when a paper cutting machine was switched on.

Mrs Annah Mathediso Maselane, an employee of South African Waste Paper Company, was on the conveyor belt which carried cardboard boxes to be sliced in the machine.

She was removing plastic which is not allowed to enter the machine.

Someone switched the machine on and Mrs Maselane was sliced in half by the cutter. She died instantly.

Detective Warrant Officer J D van Rensburg of the Potchefstroom detective branch said yesterday that an inquest will be held into Mrs Maselane's death.

The machine fused after the horribly mutilated woman entered legs first into the machine.

The matter is also to be investigated by an inspector of the Labour Department.

Mail Reporter

A woman presser operates the 'abortion machine' in a Johannesburg laundry. (1983)

Certain substances may damage an unborn child — like mercury, lead, benzine, organic dyes and radiation. Women who work in plastics, dry-cleaning and perfume factories may breathe in dangerous fumes from these chemicals. The fumes may cause a woman to miscarry, or to give birth to an abnormal baby — even if she leaves her job before the baby is born.

The South African health laws which protect a worker's health do not cover these sorts of hazards. As a result, the health of many women workers and their children may suffer.

Sexual harassment

Sexual harassment or 'love abuse' is another common problem for women factory workers. It varies from jokes and insults which men make about women workers, to acts of rape.

The letter opposite was written by a shop steward in Dunlop — a plant organised by the Chemical and Industrial Workers Union. He describes how their training officer was 'selling jobs for sex', and how the trade union got him fired. This is just one example of many instances of sexual harassment.

The stories of Mabel and Kate describe some of the different problems of women factory workers.

A WORD OF ADVICE TO OUR FELLOW BROTHERS AND SISTERS IN THE STRUGGLE

JOBS FOR SEX

This is something being done in many factories by personnel officers and training officers to our sisters, girl-friends, and wives. Managements know about it, but they don't do anything about it since it does not affect them as much as it does us workers. We keep on complaining about it, but do nothing ourselves, since our very sisters are not willing to help us out. They are afraid of victimisation and scandals. But we can still do it on our own.

How do women get trapped? Usually women get employed at factories outside working hours, even weekends. During lunchtimes you can find the personnel's office locked. But after lunch you will see a lady coming out of the very office which was locked.

At DUNLOP we realised that the training officer sold jobs for sex. From there we planned to catch him in action with workers who could walk around the offices and watch him.

He employed one lady on a Friday, and by Tuesday the following week at about 13 hrs he called the lady to his office. One of our union members rushed to the door a few minutes later to test if the door was locked or not, and found it locked. He phoned another member, who phoned one of the managers.

The training officer was caught, and got fired on the spot. The woman did not get fired.

This was far better than allowing workers to assault him as they wished. We just refused, and promised them that we would solve the problem. And now they are all happy.

(Signed)
SHOP STEWARD AT DUNLOP

Checking garments for faults
can cause eye strain.
(Knitwear factory, Johannesburg, 1981)

Cutting cloth with an unguarded blade
(Knitwear factory, Johannesburg, 1981)

Working in a clothing factory (Johannesburg, 1984)

Mabel

Mabel was a garment worker for twenty years — until she discovered that the dresses she made in one day sold for more than a week's wages.

I don't remember the year, but I left my two kids at home and went to look for a job in Parktown.

I left my children. I said to myself, "These children can talk, they can say 'I'm hungry' or 'I want to pee'. They are clever enough." So I left them with my granny and went to work.

I got a job as a domestic. I was there five years. The madam was nice, the master was nice. I liked the work.

But I left because of my grandmother. She became ill and I went to look after her. I took two weeks off. In the second week my granny passed away. There was nobody to look after my kids. I started to panic.

I started to look for a job where I could come home every night — factory work or something.

I struggled to find work. So I took some of my savings and went to an industrial school. You know, there's a school to learn sewing on industrial machines. I learnt how to use overlock, line stitch, buttonhole. I paid R25 for six months, and I learnt how to sew.

It was in the sixties — there were ten of us in the class. We got jobs in a clothing factory. I started with overlock, waistline, and sideseams.

I worked for many years — in three different clothing factories. I left my last job in 1980. This is what made me leave the job. They started to make funny ways of work — they were very strict with us.

We had to make twenty-two dresses a day. They didn't care about the patterns. If it was a difficult pattern we could only make three or four dresses a day. But they just wanted the work. If you couldn't make a large amount they would shout at you and threaten to fire you. At that time I was earning R52,95 a week.

One Tuesday we were doing tennis dresses. You know, a tennis dress is a little thing like that. And those dresses cost R59 and some coins!

Anyway those dresses were wrong — the collar. They had come from another factory. The supervisor called me. She knew: Mabel is here, Mabel can fix it quickly. She piled all the dresses in front of me.

The thing that made me mad was this. That dress was R59 and I was earning a lower wage than that dress! You know, if you were doing alterations they used to take off the price-tags. You mustn't see the price. But this time they forgot.

I started to sew — two, three, four dresses. The supervisor asked me to hurry because they were waiting for the dresses.

Oh, I was cross. I said to the supervisor, "Come here. How much is this?" and I took out my payslip. "And how much is this?" and I showed her the price-tag. And I asked, "Do you want all these dresses this week?" She said yes.

I said, "No, I'm leaving now." I didn't say anything. I just put my scissors, my tape — everything of mine — in a drawer and went out. Until today.

It's already two years. I'm at home sewing and selling what I make. I won't work in a factory again.

(Mabel was interviewed in November 1983.)

Kate Sibiya

I am a machinist — I join seat covers for motor cars. I've been doing this since 1979.

It isn't a very difficult job to do. It's quite simple. Well, it bores sometimes, when you do the same thing all along. It's better when you do this car, and then change to another car.

Since the beginning of the year we haven't worked so well. There have been lay-offs. We've only worked three months full, and the rest of the year (six months) was two days, a day, five hours or so. There's always advance warning — usually about twenty-four hours. They must call all the shop stewards in the factory and tell them there'll be a possibility of a lay-off. Then they put notices on the notice boards in the factory so that everyone can read about it.

I haven't counted up, but I think I haven't earned a third of what I'm supposed to earn this year. Because when you are on short time you don't get paid for the hours you haven't worked. It's really been a difficult time for all the workers in the motor industry.

Some of the people have got jobs in other places. But it's difficult to find a job nowadays. In fact, if there were more jobs available a lot more people would have left.

The disadvantage of working elsewhere is you won't get the amount of money that you are getting in the motor industry. It pays better than other industries. In decent times I earn R112 a week. There are lots of people in other places earning R35 a week.

Today eighty-four people were retrenched. Both men and women. In my factory we have more women than men, so always more women are retrenched. There's a possibility that there will be another retrenchment before the end of the year.

The union is quite strong in our factory — most of the workers are union members. But with the lay-offs some people want to resign, because the union didn't give them anything to live on whilst they were off work.

We want to negotiate for this supplementary unemployment fund so that if people are laid off there can be some money they get from the factory. But when I asked for it last time the personnel manager told me it would take very long — about ten years. I don't believe it, it is for us to push for it. And if we push there, it will go well.

I joined the union in 1979. But I wasn't as active as I am now. I started becoming more active three years ago when I was elected a shop steward. Then in 1982 I was elected chairperson of the shop stewards' committee in my factory.

I enjoy it very much, but it's too strenuous at my age. I'm old and I'm getting tired. I can't attend all the meetings — you know, things like that. Sometimes you sit in a boardroom for a long time — I sort of get a bit mixed up. (laughs)

Our union is recognised by management. We've got two agreements with the company — the recognition agreement and the maternity agreement.

We use the LIFO (last in first out) system for retrenchment. We tried to stop these retrenchments, but it was difficult because most of the time this year you'd get to work and sit at your machine for the whole day, doing nothing. If they don't sell anything where will the money come from to pay you? It's really tough.

Our maternity agreement is like this: a woman must have worked for eight months before going on maternity. Then she goes and she stays home for four months. When she comes back she must get the same position, or a similar one — with the same rate of pay. That four months, though, is unpaid. What we are going to try next time we negotiate is to push for payment.

My duty is to see that all the shop stewards do their duties. But it's a lot of extra work. Sometimes you're nearly off your head.

Most fortunately I have two big daughters. One looks after the children and does the housework. This leaves me free to do my union work. I've got a big family — six children, a husband and four grandchildren — who stay with me. If that daughter gets married I'll have to resign, because I will have to look after the family.

My husband encourages me. Sometimes the workers make me so cross and I just think of re-signing. Then he tells me, "Look, if you represent people you can't satisfy them all. There are those who get satisfied, and others who don't."

I worked in a pram factory for ten years before this job. I was also a machinist there. Before that I was a domestic worker — from 1949 till 1968. I used to work for these people — you know, the diplomatic corps.

What made me decide to go and work in the factory was the money. My salary as a domestic was too little, and my family was growing big.

I think factory work is much better than domestic work because as a domestic worker you are expected to work every day of your life. On a Sunday, you can't go to church, you must go to work. When you knock off, the shops are closed — you haven't got time for your shopping. You hardly have time to do washing for your own house, because you've got to work from Monday to Sunday. And on Saturday you only get off at two or three — and you still have that long journey to travel to the township.

(Kate Sibiya was interviewed in September 1984.)

4

The right to work

For the last thirty years African women have been an important part of South Africa's paid workforce. But this does not mean that they are able to get jobs when they want and need them.

It is usually the employers and the government who decide when and where women may work.

For example, thousands of African women are denied the right to work by the government's influx control laws. And those women who have jobs are often the first group of workers to be hit by retrenchments.

The end result is that unemployment among black women is very high.

Influx control

In Chapter One we saw how and why women moved into the towns to work. But at the same time the government was trying to keep women out of the towns and in the rural areas. As early as 1913 women in some areas were made to carry passes, but the women resisted this and the regulation was dropped.

By the 1930s there were laws passed again to stop women coming to town. Only women who had male relatives in town could get permission to come to the urban areas. This meant that they were forced to depend on men. They could not move freely. Once they were in the towns women were forced to depend on men for houses. It was not possible for a single woman to get a house of her own in the townships.

The authorities had their own reasons for trying to keep women out of the towns. They did not want to spend money on building houses and facilities for families.

Employers also did not want their male workers to bring wives and families to town. They preferred to employ migrant workers at low wages. They said that migrants' rural families could support themselves off the land. Employers preferred to pay a single wage rather than a family wage.

But women could not support themselves on small amounts of poor land. So the influx of black women to urban areas soared. There were no facilities for these women or their children, and huge squatter camps grew up around the cities.

Women under the pass laws
In 1948 the Nationalist government came to power and a new onslaught against black women began.

This new government did not want to have a large urban black population. They wanted the majority of people to live in the bantustans and only come to the towns to work. They knew that the more women there were in the townships, the more children would be born — and the larger the township would grow. Also, if women came to the towns families would then live permanently in the towns, and not in the reserves.

So they decided that women would have to be controlled and kept out of urban areas. Over the years they passed one law after another to keep women out of the towns.

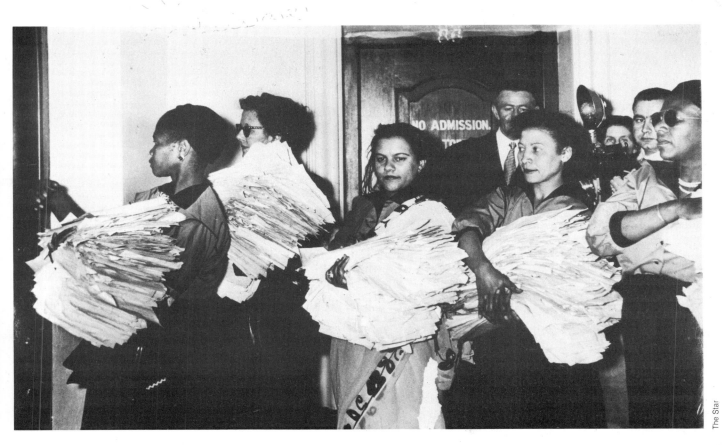

August 9, 1956. A delegation led by Lillian Ngoyi
attempts to present anti-pass petitions to the Prime Minister.
Outside, 20 000 women waited.

In 1952 the government extended the pass laws to include women. In this way they hoped to control women's movement into the towns.

Women fought hard against the pass laws. The anti-pass campaign lasted for seven years. But finally the government broke the women's resistance and by 1959 black women were forced to carry passes.

Then in the early 1960s came the next step: the government put a total ban on all rural women coming to urban areas. The only women who were legal in urban areas were the women who already had urban rights – or the women who were contract workers before this ban was introduced. Even this did not stop women coming to the towns. They wanted to escape poverty and unemployment in the bantustans. So they came illegally, and worked illegally – doing low-paid jobs like domestic work.

In 1979 influx control was tightened again. Employers would have to pay a R500 fine if they gave work to 'illegals'. Many employers complained; others just fired their illegal workers. Then the government declared a moratorium. This allowed illegal workers to register as contract workers. It meant that if these workers lost their current jobs they would be endorsed out of urban areas and would not be allowed to work there again. Even women with urban rights (Section 10(1)(a), (b) or (c)) who registered during the moratorium lost these rights and were registered as contract workers.

Divisions between women

The influx control laws have had far-reaching effects on black South African women. Influx control has divided women into two groups: urban women with Section 10 rights, who may work, and 'unqualified' women who are denied the right to work.

Urban, qualified women are more 'privileged' than their rural sisters because they have access to jobs – even though these are not likely to be very good jobs.

'Unqualified' women have the worst lives of all South Africans. They are meant to stay in the bantustans, where the land is poor and job opportunities are few. We look at the lives of these women in Chapter Five.

On 23 April 1986 the South African government abolished the influx control laws. In theory this should make it easier for black women to work legally in towns. However, the new laws will link jobs to residence in approved housing, which is in short supply in urban areas. At the time of going to press it is too soon to predict the effect of the new legislation on South Africa's black women workers.

Working illegally

Many unqualified women still come to the towns in a desperate search for jobs. They are prepared to run the risk of heavy fines and imprisonment by working illegally.

The jobs they get are very badly paid. Employers will risk fines themselves only if it means they can get cheap labour.

These women often get arrested. In 1982, 16 532 women were arrested for breaking the influx control laws.

Mildred is one of the women who is trapped in this cycle of illegal work.

Women in "men's jobs"

The influx control laws
have changed women's jobs.
More and more rural men are being
forced out of urban areas.
'Qualified' urban women
are now employed to do the jobs
of these migrant men.
Often these are heavy labouring jobs.

Mildred Mjekula

I first came to Johannesburg when I was eighteen years old in 1969. I came from Umtata in the Transkei. I have been working in Jo'burg for fifteen years, all the time without a pass because it was not easy to register.

My first job was with a Mrs Cohen, cooking and cleaning the house, and later looking after the children. Then I worked for another family, doing the same thing.

When I first worked here it was easier to work without a pass stamp. All you needed was your pass from the Transkei. But it was still difficult. My first employer used to tell me not to open the door for anybody while I was working. She tried for a long time to register me but they told her, "No chance."

I have not got a job now, and that is why I am struggling to be registered. In fact, I have been trying since 1975 to register my pass. I went to the pass office and explained that I had been working in Jo'burg for many years. But they sent me away, saying that I cannot be registered even if I get a job because I am from Matanzima. They say if you are from the homelands there is no application possible for you. At the pass office they said I should come to Black Sash — maybe they can help me.

In fact I had a job in Westcliff, but then the inspector came. That madam told me if I get registered I can come back and work for her again, because she likes me.

Since I first came to Johannesburg I have always had to look for work with a room because I have nowhere else to stay. When I look for a job I start off looking for a job in a private house, or a flat — I don't mind as long as there's a room. Usually I look in *The Star* and maybe I'll find a telephone number of people who want a maid. I phone them and then they tell me when to come so that they can see me.

While I had these domestic jobs, I used to get one off-day a week, and one weekend a month. I usually had a small room with space for a bed, a wardrobe and one small table. I started in the kitchen at 7.00 a.m. with one hour off for lunch, and then finished any time between 7.30 p.m. and 8.30 p.m. Not all employers are the same. Some do not mind visitors coming to see you. Others don't like it.

I used to get about R110,00 a month. Every month I sent my mother R60,00, sometimes less. My brother also sends her money, but I am especially strong for my mother, because my baby is there with her, and because my brothers are married already.

Six years ago I had a baby. I have only one and she stays with my mother in the Transkei. I worked while I was pregnant but I went home to give birth. Since then I only see her once a year for two weeks in December, or maybe June. I would like to have more children if I could. After my baby was born I took prevention so that I could see the first one grow. Then I stopped taking prevention but I never fell pregnant again. I went to the doctor and he told me that my tubes were blocked. One child is no good. I'd like two or three.

My child does not remember that I am her mother. She knows me, but now my mother is her mother. She doesn't love me too much and this is difficult for me. When I get a chance, I ask my mother to come to Jo'burg with her, and they stay

A Transkei family. Rural families like Mildred's
depend on money from migrant workers in town. (1981)

with me in my room. My madam didn't mind for two or three weeks, but after that she said they must go because of the inspectors.

I have a husband. At least I do not have a marriage certificate but he looks after me, so he is my husband! He is a contract worker and lives in a hostel in the township. He comes to stay with me when I have a room — perhaps for two days or a weekend, and then he goes back to the township. He comes from Tzaneen and works at a steakhouse in Rosebank.

Apart from my husband, and an uncle, it is only my younger brother here in the town. He works at the CNA, and has been in the town for ten years. He stays at Diepkloof hostel, so he can't help me with a place to stay.

My sister works as a contract worker in Cape Town. She wrote to me to tell me there is a chance now to make a contract in Cape Town. She has been working there for ten years now, and like me she has worked all the time without being registered. But I don't want to go to Cape Town.

I have a brother and a sister still living in the Transkei. It is not possible to get work in the Transkei. It is too small and there are too many people. That's why we are all coming to the town. In the Transkei you can look for work for one year and you won't find it — there's no work. People are suffering.

And even here in Johannesburg it is difficult to get work. If you are not registered the whites say they cannot take you because the inspector can come and fine them R500 and arrest you.

I have had trouble with the police before. I have been arrested three times. The first and third times I went to court and the magistrate fined me R5,00. The second time I was discharged — I don't know why.

I am afraid to walk in the streets. When the police come, they ask you for your pass and look for the stamp. Maybe you have a stamp for one year only and it is finished when the police look. They just put you in the van and take you to the police station.

If you are arrested, you can ask the police to make a phone call. You give them 30c, maybe 40c and then you can phone. I can phone my brother at work, or my husband, maybe a friend. Then they know you are in prison and they bring you food, and bail money if there is bail. If there is no bail then you can ask them to come to court with money to pay the fine.

You just sit in prison. Over the weekend — if you are arrested on Friday — it is worse. You must wait until Monday. You must wait in the same clothes, with no soap, no cream, no washing water. You are in prison with all types. Each room has fifteen to twenty people in it. Sometimes it can happen that some try to give you trouble, but if you are lucky maybe you'll find nice people to sit with. Then we look after each other and talk. I was very scared when I first went there. And later. Most of my friends have also been in prison.

Last month, while I was still struggling to be registered, I took a job at a house where the madam did not ask me if I am registered. I felt sick. I had no power and she did not like me to be sick. I said to her: "I have no power and you still want me in the kitchen. You can't even give me three days off to get a rest?" I worked until I was better, but then I left the job. I was weak and couldn't even pick up

Women wait for advice at the Black Sash. (Johannesburg, 1984)

a cup, and still she didn't give me time to rest. I could only be sick on my off-day, but I was sick before my off-day! I was cross, so I left.

I do not think it is fair that people must have a pass. They are suffering. There are many people looking for jobs. Not many have a pass and many are arrested. I do remember when women didn't have to have a pass. I remember my mother saying – I think it was 1959 – that she was going to get a pass. After that it was difficult getting jobs.

If I don't get registered I can't go back to Transkei. Maybe I will find someone nice who will take me without a stamp. But they are scared of the fine and the inspectors.

I have no other way of making money, except by working. But from now on I want to learn to do something else – maybe learn to drive or to type so that I can get a job more easily.

I don't want to live my whole life here. I want to work now while I am young but when I'm old I want to go back to Transkei.

(Mildred Mjekula was interviewed in October 1983.)

Urban unemployment

Urban, qualified women are more fortunate than 'unqualified' women, because they at least have the right to work in town. But even in urban areas unemployment among women is high.

In 1983 the government figures showed that fourteen out of every hundred black women in urban areas were unemployed. In the same year six out of every hundred urban men were unemployed. So there were more than twice as many women looking for work as there were men.

Causes
There are several reasons why women struggle to find and keep jobs.

Firstly, there are many people who think that a woman's place is in the home. They think that women only work to earn extra money – and that perhaps this is money they don't really need. This attitude is shared by the government, employers and even some of the women's men.

Secondly, as we have seen, women's jobs are usually unskilled, or semi-skilled. Most women, like domestic workers and cleaners, need very little training for their jobs. Because of this it is very easy for employers to dismiss women workers. They can easily replace one unskilled worker with another. And in times of recession unskilled and semi-skilled women workers are usually the first to be retrenched.

Thirdly, women workers often lose their jobs when they become pregnant. Even if they return to their jobs after their babies are born, their service is broken. So these women are classed as new workers, and during retrenchments, they are the first to go.

On the following page, Flora's story shows how easy it is for women to become unemployed.

Mothers take time off to care for their sick children. (Alexandra Clinic, 1980)

Flora

I was working for Star Radios. I started in 1974. It was my first job. I was young — seventeen or so.

The employer was very rude. He used to kick us. He'd say, "Do this!" and if it wasn't right he'd come and fine you — 50c fine, R1 fine — he'd take it off your wages.

I was covering the radios. It's a man's job really. They used to have four men there, but they left the job because of low wages. In 1974 I was earning R17 a week.

I left in 1976 when I got married and I went back to the same job three years later. In 1979 I was earning R45 a week.

He was a rude man, jong. If you were late he'd shout at you and lock the door — shouting, "Go to hell!" One day we did something wrong and he chased us around the factory. There were four of us girls — we ran because we couldn't wait for him to kick us.

I was working there until I had my baby. He wasn't happy about it. He shouted, "What's wrong with you?"

My baby died in January — she was only four months old. I went back to the factory but he wouldn't take me. He said, "Where the hell have you been?" He had expected me back at work after six weeks. I couldn't explain what had happened because he is a person who doesn't care about black people. He's somebody you can't tell, "My baby was ill and that's why I couldn't make it back to work." She was sick, always in the hospital.

I've never worked for anybody else. I've only worked for him. So now I'm looking for work. Any job, any job — I'll take it. Even if they say, "Come and make tea for me," I'll go because I'm stranded for work. Even if they say, "You must clean the offices," I'll go. Because I don't want to stay at home. There's no money at home — nobody gives you money.

I went to a lot of shops in town. They didn't even ask what I'd like to do — or what Standard I'd passed. I went to the OK, Edgars, I went all over. Even now I'm still asking my friends.

But domestic work — I can't do it. The money is too little. Say R50 or R100 a month. That's too little. I was working for R49 a week. It's too little.

I'll do any other job. Don't you want somebody to work for you?

My pass is okay. I was born in Johannesburg. The problem is education. We didn't have any money by the time I was at school, so I had to stay at home. They didn't understand when you said there was no money. There was no money for school fees, uniforms or even shoes. The children walked barefoot.

But I am prepared to improve myself. Maybe one day I'll be something in life. It's not too late.

(Flora was interviewed in November 1983.)

The need to work

Most working class women work because they have no option. Without their wages, they and their families would starve.

Growing numbers of black women are becoming the heads of their households. They are also the main breadwinners for their families. There are a number of reasons for this:

- In urban areas the divorce rate is increasing. Also, many women prefer to live without husbands. These women must work to support their families.
- In rural areas, large numbers of men are migrant workers. These migrants may stop sending money to their families. The women are then forced to go and look for wage-paying jobs.

Even if women are married, and live with their men, many still have to work. Their husbands may be unemployed, or they may be earning wages that are too low to support their families. An extreme example of this is farm work, where the men are paid R20 a month. In these cases every member of the family must work for the family to survive. This affects not only the women, but also children who would otherwise be at school.

Women's need to work often forces them to take very bad jobs. Some of these are described in Chapter Five. On the following pages, Alfie's story shows how her need to work forced her to take a low-paying job which is secure — rather than a better-paid but insecure factory job.

Alfie

I worked for the Hacketts for nearly twenty years. I was a little girl when I went there. I had passed Standard Five when my mother passed away. I had to leave school because there was no money and my granny was old.

My granny found this job for me in the paper. I liked it at Mrs Hackett's. She taught me a lot — she taught me to cook, wash, iron, clean, washing windows very well, and baking. And they helped me to learn English. They lived in Umkomaas.

She helped me a lot, Mrs Hackett. She used to give my granny food. I never knew what the pay was, because they used to buy food and clothes for me and my granny. Sometimes they gave me R40, sometimes R50.

Before she died Mrs Hackett told her husband to send me to sewing school. She knew if she died I wouldn't have a job, because he was on pension and couldn't afford to pay me.

So I went to the training school for six weeks to learn sewing. He paid for me — it cost R75 for the six weeks. The course was so hard, they used to use the clock: they timed everything — ten seconds, twenty seconds, everything quick, quick.

If you've got a certificate you find it easier to get a job. It's very hard without any diplomas. But if you are trained, the factory is happy to have you.

I got a job in a sewing factory in Durban. I was putting in the pockets. I worked there for eight months. At that factory I earned R26 a week. People with experience earned more — you can get R45 for long service. Then they said they were too full, they didn't have enough work. So they told me to go. They said I could come back when they were busy again.

I looked for work. I went to this shop and I met Nkosasana, and she gave me a job. I told her I knew how to sew, but not how to cut patterns. She said, "All right, I'll teach you." So now I'm making clothes. I've been here since May.

Oh, I like this job. She's teaching me to cut and I like that very much. She teaches me everything and she's not cheeky with me. If I make a mistake she talks very well.

I prefer working here to working in the factory. Because here you've got an idea. At the factory you can't cut and you can't learn how to cut. But here you can learn to make a whole dress from beginning to end.

At a factory maybe you get good money, but you can't trust the job. If there are few jobs they fire you, and when they are very busy, they want you back again. You can be working nicely and they'll tell you the job is finished. It's not right. It makes me sad. It's better if you get a little money, but you know you are working.

Here I am getting R25 a week. It's not much but it's better than the factory. If you are in a factory and they pay you R30, they take lots of money off. Also, you have to buy your own food and busfare. It's so hard. Here I'm not using the bus — only on Friday, when I go home to KwaMashu.

At home it's just me and my granny. Up to last month there were also my cousin's four children. But it was too hard for me — with me and granny and the four children and the rent. The rent there is R70 a month. It is just I who is earning. After I've paid the rent I've got R30 left. That's why I ask my aunt to take the children — because with that R30 I must buy food for my granny and myself.

Living on that R30 is hard — but it's better than not working. That time when I didn't work it was so hard. I couldn't pay for rent. There was no food. So hard. And the office came to tell me to take my clothes out of the house. I hadn't paid the rent for three months. So very hard.

Every weekend I go to KwaMashu. I get there at about nine o'clock on Friday night. My granny is there by herself all week. I don't like it when people come and visit my granny because they want to eat all her food. They say they want tea, coffee, rice. No. I don't like it, I'll tell you true. She just gives it to them, ja. Sometimes I go home and there's no food at all. I tell her please, it's too expensive.

She likes visitors, and she's stupid because she gives them food. If she goes to visit them, they don't give her anything. Not even tea.

I'm not married. I'm afraid to get married. My granny didn't want me to, but I also don't like marriage. Because men are so hard when you are married. Men drink and they hit you. I see it everywhere. Like my neighbours next door. Last year they got married, this year they are divorced. And it's so hard for the children — they have no father. I don't like men. Life would be harder if I was married — yes.

I've got no friends, only the church. I don't like making friends. People talk too much. I don't like to talk — I shut my mouth.

Ja, my granny's very old. She could go anytime. And then — then I must just stay alone.

(Alfie was interviewed in August 1984.)

Self-employed women

What happens to the many thousands of women who need to work, but who cannot get jobs? Many of them work at home in jobs they have created for themselves. They do work like child-minding, beer-brewing, sewing, selling, prostitution and running shebeens.

Some women, like Elsie (page 35) prefer to be self-employed because they can earn more than they would as wage workers. But most self-employed women do this because they have no choice.

Self-employment can be the most difficult work of all. Most women earn very little, and their work is insecure. Many of these jobs are illegal — for example hawkers run the risk of high fines and imprisonment. There is also no protection in the cases of sickness, maternity or old age.

Work like selling and brewing is also hard and tiring. Women often have to travel long distances to buy the raw materials for their trade. And they make little profit.

These jobs are often done by women who cannot work legally in urban areas. Agnes's story, below, speaks for many self-employed women who are 'illegal' in town. Dolly took on extra work when her husband went to jail. Soon she found that she could earn more being self-employed than by working in a factory.

Ciskie Tilo, shebeen queen (Soweto, 1985)

Agnes Thulare

For two years I've been living in Soweto and selling fruit and vegetables. There is a group of us who sell together. We don't sell in one place — we move around.

I stay in a shack in some people's backyard. My family are not here with me. They are in Bushbuckridge. My three children are there also.

The people I live with are kind, and I am quite happy with them. I pay R3 a week rent. It is not difficult to afford.

I don't have a licence to sell fruit and vegetables but I think you can get them from the local West Rand Board office. Once we went there to apply and they told us, "You don't qualify for permits because your passes are not from Johannesburg." So I gave up trying.

I buy my fruit and vegetables three times a week. On Tuesdays and Fridays I catch a train to Faraday to buy things. On Wednesdays I go to the Kliptown market. I like to compare the different prices. That way I am able to save myself a few cents. Every cent counts a lot.

I usually spend about R30. Market prices differ a lot. You may find a box of tomatoes at R1,80 in town — but the same may cost R2,50 in Kliptown. Most of the time we sell at the same prices. We sell our vegetables in plastic bags to keep them fresh and tasty. We usually charge 30c for a bag of tomatoes, 35c for onions and 50c for potatoes.

Business is better at the end of the month. But there are so many of us selling the same kind of vegetables that we don't make such a fortune. Not all days are the same, but on a good day I make R16.

What can we do? We are all very poor. As long as we can eat, pay our rent and send some money home to our people, then all is well.

Back home in Bushbuckridge there is no money at all. It's hard life out there. Even the cows are dying because of the drought. And there is no food.

Apart from my children there are five in the family. But my brothers and sisters are unemployed. They help in the fields, but that doesn't mean that they have a job. My parents are now too old to work. They don't even have a pension. So they depend on me for support.

I am the only one who sends money to the family. Though I do not make much, I still manage to send my children to school. They never go hungry. I usually send money once a month — sometimes I visit them also.

My children are fatherless. All that men know is to leave us holding babies in our arms. They run away from their responsibilities.

I can't take my husband to court to get money. It would not be wise — they might send him to jail. As soon as he comes back he might try and kill the children so that he doesn't have to pay.

It's best if I take care of my children and look after them until they are big enough. Some day they will also look after me. I don't care for that good-for-nothing man. Even if he marries another woman, I don't care!

Selling vegetables is strenuous work, but there is nothing better I can do. The only other job I've had was in a factory. It was near Sabie. I worked on a machine that cuts wood. We didn't get enough money — money is scarce in the country. All we got was R22 a month. I worked there for a year. Then my employer called me to the office and told me there was no more work. That's why I left the job.

I can't say that I like this job, or that I don't like it. At least I know that every cent I make is mine. If you work for a white employer he may offer you a new uniform when you have worked well, instead of giving you extra money. I call that cheating.

The other good thing in this job is that you can always take your baby to work with you. Look over there — there goes a hawker with her baby on her back. You just can't do that if you work for a white employer in town.

If I could get a better job I wouldn't hesitate to leave. But my reference book isn't right for Johannesburg — so I can't find a better way of earning a living.

(Agnes Thulare was interviewed in September 1983.)

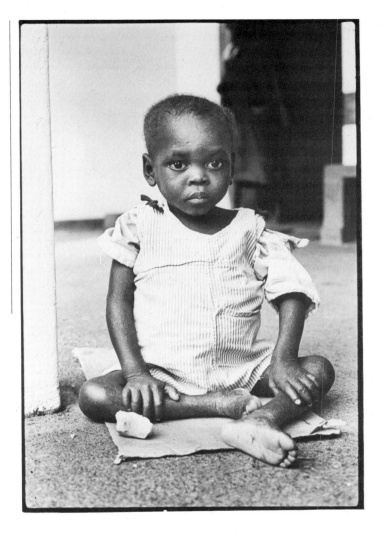

Malnourished child (Gazankulu, 1980)

89

Vegetable vendors (Orlando, Soweto, 1984)

Dolly

When Dolly's husband went into jail in the early 1960s she was forced to do extra work to support her two children. She chose prostitution. Twenty years later she describes what this job has done for her.

I started working in a glove factory in 1959. The money was so little, and I just couldn't bring up my children. Between 1961 and 1963 my husband was going in and out of jail, for theft.

I became a prostitute through circumstances. I was struggling. Most of the time I had to borrow money. People in the factory would say, "Oh, here she comes again...." You have to beg for food. What will the children eat? If there's a way out, make use of it.

One night I said, "To hell with everything. I'm not going home tonight. I must make some money." That's when I started. I met a man and he gave me some money. I went home and fed my children, and went back to work again. Then it became a habit.

When my husband came back from jail he said that my second daughter was not his. I said, "Okay, seeing as the second one is not yours, I'll take them both and bring them up myself."

In 1964 I went on a whoring spree. I kept on working in the factory for a few years, but this prostitution paid me more than my job. A lot more. You could make R80 to R100 a night. They used to pay a lot of money.

You know, these days things ain't what they used to be. Today there's the cops, today there's the customer who tells you he's only got R2 on him. I mean, what can you do with that? Today a penicillin injection costs R5. I mean you've got to look after your health at the same time.

Since there are these young girls coming up, they don't pay anymore. They rather tell you, "Get me a young girl." At times they give you R10, R5, R2. Some of them they just take you and dump you right out in the veld when they've had you. Then you are told, "F . . . off, you black bitch." And you must just go. Who wants to get hurt? But if you get a chance, once he's drunk, you just pick-pocket him.

Before it was easier. We used to queue up in Edith Cavell and Bree. There were about ten of us.

The police were not so inquisitive then. There was a place where we used to go — some offices with toilets and bathrooms. We had some pieces of cardboard. It paid, man. Jesus Christ, you can go twelve times in one night! (*laughs*) Stamina!

The next day you feel nothing. Practically nothing. You must just get your injection.

Once I came across a man who was so drunk. I took him to the building and I asked, "How much?" And he said, "No, I'll give you R10 and if it's good I'll give you R15." And then he took out of a bundle of R10 notes — so thick — and I must get one ten rand out of that! I thought okay, I'll fix him up.

So while he was lying there I just went for those R10 notes in his pocket. I put the money under my armpit, and he didn't see. You know, that day I ran all the way to Commissioner Street without my panties on!

These days I don't go round like I did before. I mean, at forty-two? You know one gets tired of lying on your back every five minutes. Ooh, honestly. Unless I've got an appointment with someone I know. I go to his flat on a Sunday morning, or Saturday afternoon. But not at night because it's risky — the police this side, the muggers that side.

I used to operate in Hillbrow a lot. But nowadays I haven't got a place to go to during the day. You've got to go maybe in a passage. It's risky.

It's very risky. Prostitution is not nice at all. It pays . . . it does not pay. No.

I've been caught twice before. The second time it was 1979, I think. I was on trial for three weeks and I got nine months for soliciting.

Oh well, once you're used to jail, there's nothing

wrong. You just do everything they tell you to do if you don't want to be punished. That's all. I was in the Fort here, and then we went to Boksburg. After a few months they sell you — you can work for some whites.

I went with a gang to Brits. Now those are farms! Phew! From 7 a.m. till 8 p.m. you worked. Oh, it was strenuous. We were sowing, reaping, irrigating, doing a lot of things, man. We were being paid maybe 20c a day.

The conditions were horrible. Jesus Christ. The huts, they were so small — and there were four or five of us in there. No curtains, no windows and muddy. They gave you a blanket and two sacks.

In the morning you ate tea and porridge. Lunchtime — spinach and porridge. Suppertime — tea and porridge. Unless you had money and could buy yourself something else.

I was bitten by a dog and they just used some plaster and grease. And I had to work with that, you know. It was painful. When I came out of jail I went straight to the hospital. It was septic, smelling.

Since then I've been to jail for a reference book, trespassing — but not immorality or soliciting. No, I go carefully with it. I have an appointment, I know where to go and I'm careful.

Now I'm not earning enough. I'm looking for a job actually. Domestic, or floor cleaning — as long as I can work. I'm not choosy you know, as long as I can make ends meet. At forty-two, who wants to go to jail again? I'm too old for whoring. It's not life. Not at all.

This prostitution frightens me nowadays. From 1964 — this is my twentieth year. It's a long time. My children are grown up. I'm a granny now.

My daughters went to Botswana long ago. They've both matriculated. One is an accountant in a bakery, the other works in a bank as a teller. I mean they're twenty-three and twenty-one this year. They don't help me, you know what children are — they just want beautiful things and everything.

I don't like to see their father. He always wants them to come to him, now they are big. I don't mind, no hard feelings — as long as he doesn't bother me. What I don't like is whenever he comes across me he says, "Do you still sell your body?" I say, "It brought your children up. Never you mind selling it. Today you are proud of them." He didn't support them at all. You can just believe me.

Now he's selling drugs. I hope he gets caught, honestly. He's so well-off — he's got a Mercedes, he's bought a big house. But I don't want his wealth. I'll keep my poverty with pride.

Most prostitutes have no choice. Especially if you're the only breadwinner. You've got to pay rent, food and everything. You become a prostitute through circumstance.

Most of the men in Soweto are so useless. I don't know why, they're not prepared to work. They just sit around in the house and do nothing.

It's mostly white men I go with. I don't feel anything for them . . . pay me first! But once they are used to you they take advantage. Acting as if they haven't got money, or just dumping you in the veld. It's heartbreaking. We are not inhuman. We've got feelings too.

(Dolly was interviewed in September 1984.)

Rural women

5

Today there are more women than ever who are trapped in the rural areas. Because of the influx control laws, they have no rights to work in the towns.

According to government policy these women should be able to survive by farming small plots of land. But land is scarce — and what land there is, is poor. So in order to survive the women have to depend on relatives earning money in the towns. Or they have to find work.

The most common jobs in rural areas are ones on white-owned farms and in bantustan industries or projects. All these jobs involve heavy work and are badly paid. And there aren't enough of them for all the people who need work.

In this chapter we will look at the working lives of the women who are forced to live in the rural areas.

Agricultural workers

The government figures show that more than one out of every three black working women are agricultural workers. By agricultural work they mean farming on one's own land or doing work for wages on somebody else's farm.

Farming has become more and more difficult in the bantustans. Many black people classified as agricultural workers are hardly able to farm at all. These women are actually unemployed.

They struggle to survive on money sent to them by migrant workers, or on old age pensions. Both these incomes are unreliable. Migrants may stop sending money (as in the case of Ma Dlomo, page 103), and pensions are often not paid out. In KwaZulu for example, no new pensions were given in 1983 because so many pensions were still owing from previous years.

Some women try to keep themselves alive by making and selling things like baskets, or by hawking. Many rely on neighbours who are prepared to lend them food or money.

Farm labourers

The women who work for wages on someone else's farm are not much better off.

Farm work has always been one of the lowest-paying jobs. It is quite common for a farmer to pay a worker R20 and a bag of mealie meal per month.

Like domestic workers, farm workers have no protection from the law — no minimum wages, no fixed hours of work and no guaranteed holidays. It is common practice for a farmer to expect workers to work six full days a week — and not to have paid holidays.

Changes in government policy have made the position of farm workers even worse.

Up until the 1960s farm workers were employed on the labour tenancy system. This meant that they lived as families on the farm. The farmer gave them fields

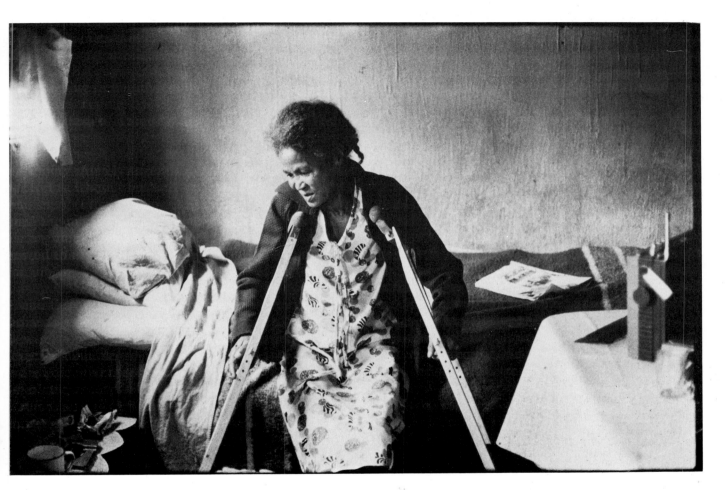

Farm worker with a broken leg. She gets no pay while she's off work. (Western Cape, 1983)

Women work in the clinic vegetable garden. (Gazankulu, 1980)

to plough and they were able to keep cattle and goats, etc. For six months of the year they did their own farming, and for six months of the year they worked for the farmer for a wage.

Then the government abolished the labour tenancy system. Thousands of farm workers were thrown off white farms. Between 1960 and 1980 one and a quarter million people were evicted. Many ended up in the bantustans. The few workers who were needed all year round were allowed to stay. But they were no longer allowed to plough or keep large numbers of cattle.

Grape picking — an example of unskilled, seasonal work (Western Cape, 1983)

Seasonal workers

Now, when farmers need extra workers — for example during the harvest — they employ seasonal or casual labourers. This kind of work is insecure and very badly paid. Increasingly it is desperate women and children from the bantustans who are doing this kind of work. Wages are as low as 80c a day. Some farmers only pay in kind! A woman may work for a whole day for a bucket of tomatoes. At the end of the day she will have to work again to sell the tomatoes to get money.

The interviews which follow describe the hardship of rural women's lives.

Farm worker's family. On this farm workers earn R180 a year. (Piet Retief area, 1982)

Rose

Rose is unemployed, living in Lebowa. She explains how her life changed when the government started planning the area. (This kind of planning is called betterment. Betterment has taken land or cattle away from many rural people.)

I am unemployed at the present time. I want to work but I can't find any. I was born on a white man's farm. We left the farm at the end of 1973 when the farmer moved away. This was the last time I worked.

Chief Pasha took over the area after the farmer left, and we were then incorporated into this tribal authority. Since then, because of the planning system, the amount of land we have has decreased. Before planning, we could plough as much as we wanted. It is the agricultural department that plans. They have not worked with us.

We were staying outside this residential area and so we had to move when the lines were cut. It was painful because the house I built was expensive and I got no compensation. But I had to oblige. We also had to get rid of our cattle because the planning system did not want them. We took them to our relatives, but they died.

Now we have no ploughing fields. We are dying of hunger. Once the agricultural officers called us together to teach us how to farm, but this never happened again. They told us to buy fertilizer, but it costs R7 or more a bag, and us starving people, we have no money.

Things will only get worse, because once an area is planned we can't live as we wish, and chop wood where we want. So we have to cook with coal, and this costs R4 a bag — and it only lasts us one week.

The planning rules also stop us from cutting down young trees. They say we must use dead wood for fires, but where is the wood? There are no trees here.

Now that we live here we have to buy everything that we need. Things will only get worse, because these prices — they go up from day to day. We don't have money anymore to buy clothes, or look after the children.

We aren't the only ones. Everyone around here is the same. It's so bad, there are as many people who don't have land as those who do. Only the people who've already paid all the fees for schools and residence plots get land to farm. And costs are so high — it's R40 for school, R2 for water, R1 for the plot — who can pay?

We grow mealies, watermelons, pumpkins and beans around the house. But it isn't nearly enough to feed us and so we have to buy our food from the shop. We also have three chickens. Sometimes we get eggs. But the chickens are thin, so mostly not.

There are seven of us — me, my husband and my five children. They're at school, but if things stay so bad some will have to leave. My husband works at the ferro-chrome mine. I don't know how much he earns. He doesn't give me any cash, he only buys what he thinks is necessary. Often there is no money in the house. When this happens I borrow from the neighbours. People here are good. They do lend money if they have. We have helped each other. It's all there is.

(Rose was interviewed in 1981.)

Ma Dlomo Lugogo

Ma Dlomo Lugogo is a widow living in Mehloloaneng village, Transkei.

I was born in this place, at the mission. That was in 1931.

I only went to school for a little bit. I've got Standard Two. Why? Because in my home there was nobody to look after the cattle, sheep and horses. So I had to go and be a shepherd.

We had a lot of cattle. I can't remember how many but there were a lot – and seven horses. But they are all dead now.

I got married in 1950. My husband's father rented a place near here because there was good grass and water for his cattle. He had a good farm in those days. My husband was working and he used to send me some money. We had four children – two boys and two girls.

Life was better in those days. We were ploughing mealies. We had two places where we could plough, but the government took away one field. Even now we've still got that other field, but because of the drought we get nothing from it.

My husband died in 1960. There was an accident on the road. He was digging and he got killed by the machine that builds the roads. They gave me a very little bit of money. It didn't take a year, and the money was finished. We were paying taxes, but the government didn't help me. The money they gave was too little – and yet he was working for the government.

The load was heavy for me. My husband's brother took away my son to go and stay with him in Mount Fletcher. He saw I was struggling to bring up all these children. And he didn't have any sons – so he took him in.

I went to work on a farm near Harding. My brother was the induna there, and he called me. We were planting trees. I used to get R15 a month. But it was worth a lot more because the prices were not so high. I left that place because it was raining all the time.

Once I went to Johannesburg to work. I was employed in a shop in Kliptown. My job was to take fruit and veggies out into the street and sell them. The money was much better than I got at Harding.

I liked it in town – it was very nice. But I couldn't speak all the languages that other people spoke. I like staying here because we understand each other.

I went back home because my daughter was going to have a baby, and there was nobody to look after the children. That's what keeps me here – my children and my grandchildren. If I didn't have children I would stay in Johannesburg and not come back.

Now I am living here with my son, Sibininiza. I am trying to make a nice vegetable garden, but I haven't got the strength. I used to grow pumpkins and a few things, but now I want to have a proper garden. I am interested because there are people here who explain how to grow spinach and all sorts of other things.

It's difficult but I am trying hard. I haven't got enough in my garden because this year I planted late. And a hailstorm came and destroyed everything. So I can't live off it.

I just live, I don't know how I manage. But I do

eat. My one daughter is a domestic worker in Pieter-maritzburg and she usually sends me money. But now there is a big delay. She hasn't sent me any money for five months and she's the only person I get money from. It's hard because I have to go to my neighbours and ask them for mealie meal.

My other daughter is married, and she doesn't work, so she can't support me. And my other son is still at school in Mount Fletcher.

I've got no cattle, but I do have about six chickens. They are busy hatching eggs, so I'm not eating eggs. I've got eight goats, and I get milk from them when the grass is green. But now they are starving and I don't get enough milk.

Mostly I eat mealie meal porridge and tea. Sometimes there's imifino, but usually there's nothing else to eat. I'm putting all my hopes in the vegetable garden. I hope I can grow enough to sell.

Life here is hard, but not for everybody. For those who have got food and money, it's not so hard. You need money to live here. I can't garden without money to buy seeds and things for the farm.

It is easier for a woman to survive than a man. There are a lot of little things you can do — you can make beer, or look after your neighbour's children. You can plant turnips, peas, beetroot with your own hands, and sell them.

But if a man can't find work he's finished. Unless he knows about carpentry and someone will pay him to build their house — or somebody will pay him to take out their cattle.

The only work that a man will do around here is to get up and go and take the cattle to the veld. If you ask him to make the fire, he'll say no, he won't do that.

After he's taken the cattle, you see him sitting in the sun with a big dish of food. Besides that, all he knows how to do is to get up and go and look for beer. I don't see a man doing anything at home. No, nothing.

I sometimes cut grass out in the fields and make it into bundles. I sell these bundles of grass for thatch — it's R20 for a hundred bundles. There are many women who do this. I do it because I'm all alone. But women with husbands do it, and the husbands don't help. They just stay at home. If the husband helped his wife they could earn more than that R20. But you'll never see a man there where we cut the grass. It's only women.

I think some men are lazy. When a child grows up and begins to work, the man will come to you and tell you, "This is my child." He wants the child to support him. But when you struggled to support that child he was doing nothing.

I used to be a big, healthy woman. But now I am getting sick and thin. I have got no aches or pains, but what worries me is that I have sleepless nights. I don't know why I can't sleep, but sometimes I stay awake the whole night, without even dreaming. If I was somebody that drank beer, I would drink so much that I would sleep straight away. But I don't drink.

Last summer, I was struck by lightning. I didn't see or hear anything. All I remember is that I was watching the rain and hail come down. I was sort of unconscious. People tell me that they found me lying on the floor. The chair I had been sitting on was on top of me. I think that chair did a good job that day, because the centre pole of the house was shattered to pieces. The whole roof would have fallen on me.

I was lucky to be found alive, because after that the lightning struck my neighbour, and she was killed. Their whole house burnt down. I was lucky to survive.
(Ma Dlomo Lugogo was interviewed in August 1984.)

Ma Dlomo Lugogo with her grandchild next to her vegetable garden

Alice and her husband, retired farm workers

Alice

Alice is a retired farm worker in the Piet Retief area. She comments on how life has changed since the labour tenancy system ended. One of Alice's sons works on the farm where they now live. Her other children work on the East Rand.

I don't know when I was born. My mother never told me!

The wages here are R20 a month. We survive because we are helped by our children in the location. Without them, I don't know. There is a farm on that side where the white man pays the people R10 a month. No, what can they eat? How can you live? And children too. That white man is playing with people – R10 a month! For men!

The whites have money. Really and truly they have lots. They have cars and lorries and aeroplanes. And what can we buy? Nothing. We must all get a little strength. All people must have something.

The workers must get up at five o'clock in the morning and they get back late. Look now, they are still not back and it is Saturday afternoon. Why must they work on a Saturday afternoon – people who live and were born here? Is it a punishment?

This R20 of theirs is ridiculous. They must know how much sugar costs. I go to the shop here, and it is the same price for everyone. Poor people don't pay less. And the price here is not the same as it is in town. All things here are crooked. They cheat us. They make sugar more expensive here because the next shop is far.

We have always suffered on the farms, but things were better before. Before, we could plough. Our parents worked on the six month system. But they ploughed and they got mealies. Now things have changed. They don't want you to plough, and yet the money is too little.

We have a few cattle that we have raised. But we are not allowed to raise many. We ourselves have twenty-one cattle. We just keep quiet about it, and the whites keep quiet. But over on that side the farmers pay R10 and they only allow seven cows. Jesus, you don't know what the whites around here are like.

If people have no children in Jo'burg what will they eat? It's because of this that some of the children are swollen up. Yes, they swell up and die from hunger.

They changed the system three years ago. Why? We don't know. They said, "The thing of six months is finished. Instead we will pay you money." Pay how much? R10? Whoo!

If all our children go for better work in Jo'burg they will fire us from here. We will have to go to the reserves. That place is terrible. It's all hills. Even a car can't drive there. It's full and full of stones. People go there. What else can they do? They say that they are starving. Oh Jesus, there is famine there.

I was born on a farm near here. At that place we earned nothing. It was the six month system. Could you do that work Nkosasana? Yes, and now we are old, what will we get? Those boers who used us for free – what will they do for us now that we are old? Nothing, niks.

(Alice was interviewed in April 1982.)

Bantustan factory workers

Some rural women work in bantustan factories under conditions that are almost as bad as those of the farm workers.

Bantustan factories are not covered by the laws which protect factory workers in the towns. For example there are no legally set minimum wages. This allows factory owners in these areas to pay very low wages. There have been cases where women were earning R8 a week.

Bantustan factory workers are not covered by the Basic Conditions of Employment Act which sets minimum working conditions. Also, many factory workers in the bantustans are prevented from joining trade unions. Bophutatswana has banned all South African trade unions and in the Ciskei SAAWU (The South African Allied Workers Union) is banned.

So bantustan factory workers are the least protected of all factory workers.

Figures from 1976 showed that more than half of bantustan factory workers were women. (These were figures for Lebowa, Venda, Ciskei and Bophutatswana.) Most men were able to get jobs as migrant workers in factories in the towns. It is desperate unemployed women, who have no choice, who do these bantustan factory jobs.

Gugu Mhlongo

Gugu is one of the top-paid workers at a textile factory in Isithebe, KwaZulu. She stays in this job because she has not got the legal right to work elsewhere.

I am a superintendent and I am responsible for the workers. I report all grievances to management, and anything else that goes wrong.

I am qualified in the textile industry. In 1981 I worked in one of the factories here in Isithebe and they trained me. It was a six-month training course. We got paid R18 a week. Then they gave me a card that says I'm qualified to do this job. They say they are training me so that if I go to another factory in Tongaat or Durban I will get a good wage.

Now I am earning R38 a week. Another woman and myself earn the same — we are the top-paid workers in the factory. There are mostly women in this place and they earn very low wages.

I would like to go to a better place to work but I don't have any rights to work anywhere else. Also, I have to look after my mother. I am the only one who helps her. I've got a brother, but he got lost in 1979. He went to Stanger and he never came back. Rumours say that he is alive and living in Johannesburg.

Our main problems at work are that we are working very hard. If one asks for the workload to be reduced, that person who asks is dismissed instantly. Six or seven women have been dismissed for this reason. Also the wages are very low — it's a big problem.

Another thing, when you go on holiday you don't get proper leave pay. If you get R18 a week, you will get R13 leave pay and no bonus.

Gugu and friend, Bantustan factory workers

I have worked in three factories in Isithebe and they are all identical. You see that the factories are very beautiful and smart. It's because we are working so hard. Their profits are unbelievable.

Now I am interested in joining the Textile Union. I have seen some factories here who have joined the union. If they ask for improvements they get what they want. In fact, even if a person makes a mistake she is not dismissed like a dog. We haven't heard much yet, but the little we know is enough. We know very well it is going to bring a change to the work situation.

I think that the coming of the factories here was a good thing. Things are selling around here much cheaper than before. But the wages and working conditions are terrible.

There are many who say that these factories are better than nothing. I agree. It would be bad if they closed down. It would be worse if there was nothing.

(Gugu Mhlongo was interviewed in August 1984.)

6

The
double
shift

Pauline, domestic worker
(Johannesburg, 1984)

◄ At work   At home ►

Women workers do two jobs. They work for wages during the day, and they do domestic work for their families at night and on the weekends. This second job at home is not usually seen as proper work — and it is not paid. But society depends on this second 'shift'. If there was no one to do this work, industry and society would break down. Workers need clothing and regular meals, otherwise they would not be able to do their jobs. Children need to be properly cared for so that they can grow up into healthy adults. Families need reasonably clean places to live in, or else they would get sick.

Connie Radebe prepares the evening meal for her family.
During the day she works as a canteen cook. (Soweto, 1985)

The Legal and General Insurance Company estimated in 1982
that the commercial value of work a wife does in the home as cook,
childminder, nurse is £204 (about R500) per week.

From the British Trades Union Council book 'Working Women'.

Very few men will share this domestic work, because they see it as 'women's work'. So women have no choice but to do it. Food has to be cooked and children and husbands have to be clothed.

This second job is heavy and demanding — especially after a long day at work and hours of travelling. Women workers have little time to rest, see friends, or participate in community and trade union activities. The health of many women workers suffers from stress and overwork.

Night shift workers suffer even more. Women who work at night arrive home in time to make breakfast for their families. After cleaning the house and shopping there are only a few hours left to sleep before the family returns from school or work. Interviews with night cleaners in Johannesburg showed that two out of three workers slept less than four hours a day. Most of these women complained of health problems such as sore eyes, headaches, backache, sore legs, and sore stomach and high blood pressure. The stories of Nomvula (page 21) and Maureen (page 51) describe what life is like for night shift workers.

Childcare is another major problem for working women. In 1983 some researchers talked to women shop workers and clothing workers in Johannesburg. They found that most of these women had babies and children. Most of the women had to go back to work after their babies were born — when the babies were younger than a year old.

There are not enough creches in the townships. In Soweto, for example, the creches can only take six out of every one hundred children who need day care. So most working mothers have to send their babies to child-minders.

This can be a source of great worry for working mothers. Many child-minders struggle to give children proper care. They are usually old and not very strong. Often mothers spend their working days worrying about their children. Also, child-minders cost money. The average cost in Soweto is R25 a month for one child. And this is a lot of money for the mothers to pay since they themselves are badly paid workers.

Many women — whether single or married — are the heads of their households. Even if husbands work they seldom tell their wives what they earn, and the husbands decide how much to contribute to the household. Yet it is the women who make sure that the family is clothed and fed. Single women have to bear this burden alone.

Many of the women who have spoken in this book have mentioned the difficulty of having two jobs. Rose's baby (see page 10) died because of inadequate childcare when she was at work. Kate (page 70) says she would have to ditch her union responsibilities if she had to do the housework. Elsie (page 37) says she feels like 'the girl' in her own home.

On the following pages, Thembi, Anna and Louise talk in more detail about the double shift.

Thembi Nabe

Thembi is an organiser in MAWU (Metal and Allied Workers Union). She gave her views on the double shift at a talk on women workers in July 1983.

Both man and wife have to get up in the morning to work. But the woman has to get up first; make tea for her husband, prepare water to wash, make the bed while the man is still washing; wash the baby and take it to the nurse lady who looks after it. Then she comes home and prepares herself to go to work.

But remember the woman works as a domestic, harassed by the madam during the rest of the day. Or she works in a factory. Long hours. Hard work. She finishes work at 5.30 p.m. and then she has to travel from work to home. The earliest she can get home is 7.30 p.m.

The husband finishes work at 5.00 p.m. at a Germiston foundry and gets home at 6.30 p.m. at the latest. When he gets home he doesn't make a fire to warm the house; he will just put on the heater, sit next to it and read the paper, watch TV, or play horses. He doesn't fetch the baby. He

doesn't look after it. You know, he makes a point that every time when he comes back from work, there's his 'little darling' next to him, which is a bottle of whisky or brandy.

On the way home from work the woman will fetch the child. When she gets home she makes the fire, starts preparing the evening meal, then washes the child, and feeds it, and then prepares the bed for the husband. The woman must do everything – see to it that tomorrow she doesn't have too much work to do because she must carry the baby and prepare every-thing. Most women do their ironing during the night.

And when it comes to bedtime, the husband becomes impatient if the woman does not come to bed when he calls her. When she does go to bed – there starts another overtime! But if she is tired and refuses him, that is the beginning of another problem. He becomes a cheeky somebody. And sometimes because of his 'little darling' which was on the table, he thinks of battering you. Or he will go out and find another woman. And that is where divorce begins.

Anna

Anna lives in Driefontein which is a 'black spot', doomed to be relocated. Her husband Timothy is paralysed and unable to help himself in any way. He has been like this since April 1982 when his employer's truck overturned on him and eighteen other farm workers. His neck was broken in the accident and one other farm worker died. Since the accident Timothy has had no help from the farmer. He only received R329 from Workmen's Compensation. This means that Anna has to work to support him and their two children. She is also responsible for all the domestic work at home. Their house is collaps-

ing, and this too she must rebuild. It is a mud house and must be completed quickly as the mud washes away every time it rains.

We're really struggling because we don't even have enough mealie meal. The money I get from the white man I work for is only R30 a month. And that is if you've been to work every day. If you miss one day, or you loaf for one day he cuts off a lot of that money. So that salary is R30 and one gogok (*20 litre tin*) of mealie meal.

At work we have to take some of that mealie meal and cook it for ourselves. He doesn't give us any extra food there.

I've been working in the forests for about a year. And even before my husband had his accident I used to work sometimes.

We start work at 7 a.m. I wake up very early and then I've got to fix up my husband. Because I know that the first time he'll eat is when I come home in the evening. So I try to make him something that he can keep during the day. But often I don't have time because I'm rushing so much in the morning. I also have to get my children ready for school. If I don't have time to get anything ready for him, the first meal he will have will be late in the evening.

In the morning we're fetched by a truck that takes us to work. It comes to fetch us down at the butcher in the middle of Driefontein. Quite a few of us — men and women — wait for it there every morning. This truck starts here in Driefontein with us and then goes and picks up some other people from the farms. I leave home at a quarter to six and I get to the butchery at half past six. That is when the truck comes to fetch us.

We knock off at five. But then there's the journey back and I have to walk home, so I get home at about half past six. I am very tired by the time I get home because I know that things are just beginning then. Because I still haven't got water, I still haven't got wood. I must still do all of those things.

The first thing I do is I try and get firewood, because you know that here in Driefontein we have to buy firewood — and I don't have money for such things. So I have to go and steal wood from the white people's forests which are quite far. It's a very dangerous thing to steal that wood. When I've got the wood and I'm safely home I start making the fire.

My children are too young to do these things. So even fetching water I have to do myself. It will be better when they grow up and they can help me.

I always feel tired and sick, because there are so many things that I have to do all the time. I never rest. Every morning I wake up late. I'm tired, because the night before I've gone under the fences to steal firewood, and I've watched out for the GGs (*the government*). If I see cars then I have to come back slowly in the dark with the wood. I have to wait to see that they've gone before I can come back.

The other thing that I'm doing now is building a house. And I really can't manage. Because all week I am working and I have to build on Saturdays and Sundays only.

And I'm working all by myself building this house. Putting on the mud and trying to steal those long poles which I have to bring back on my head. There's no one to help. Anyone who'll help, I'll have to pay. In fact I asked them and they said that. They said they needed the money. There's only one brother who sometimes helps us. That's all, he's the only one. The others, anything they do they want money for.

The two children are at school now. Before we had to take them out of school because there was no money. Then the church came to help us with money. Even now, though, it's difficult because at school they need many things. They're always asking for money but we can't give them those things. That priest gave us R50 to send the children back to school. And I got one shirt for my son and one shirt for my daughter and a few other things and the money was finished. Books they have to borrow, and they still have no shoes. They have to walk that

Gazankulu, 1980

long distance every day without shoes.

We can never eat meat. Just mealie meal and milk from our cow. Before, we sometimes used to have chicken. But then all my chickens died because no one was at home to look after them. Sometimes we eat imifino, but now there is none.

(Anna was interviewed in April 1983.)

Travel adds hours on to a woman's double day. (Natal, 1984)

Louise Yekwa

Louise is a school teacher in Alexandra. As a teacher, her working hours are short. But Louise is also studying for her matric — so she has three shifts.

Now I'm teaching in Alex. I'm teaching higher primary — general science and health education, Afrikaans and needlework. Ooh, it's demanding. But I like teaching. As compared with other jobs there are some advantages. Because you knock off at about ten past two. Then if you've got some work to do you remain until three o'clock, then you can go home, look after the kids. You've got to take them from creche.

When I get home from school I do some ironing, sweep and dust the house. And then I start cooking.

At home I don't have anyone to help me. I have to do everything because my kids are still young. When I'm not at home my husband helps. When I'm at home — nothing. He only cooks when I am out — maybe if I'm away on a school tour. But he'll never cook when I'm around. The thing is, he's studying and he wants time to read.

I'm studying for matric because I want to get promoted. I don't want to become a principal. I just want to be an inspectress. That's what I'm aiming at.

I study after supper. I forget about TV and the radio. Then I sit on my books. Sometimes I sleep early. I go to sleep at eight o'clock and wake up at about twelve and study till morning. It's easier to work when everybody's sleeping. I can't make it during the day.

When I was doing teacher training one of my teachers used to say, "The problem with you women

is, you like to sweep your houses so that they are spick and span. How about if you sweep your houses maybe three times a week and go on with your books?"

And I thought, no, I don't know what to do. The house must be swept, the washing must be done — and I must cook and wash the dishes.

So I decided to work at night. I started this last year in about September. At first I was feeling tired, but then I just got used to it. I know if I do this for a few years then for the rest of my life I can sleep as much as I like.

I don't see people very often. My neighbours tell me, "Ooh, you're so scarce." I just meet them when I go to the shop, or maybe going to school. I have got friends, but no one special. I don't see my family very often because they are far away. Except for my mother. She's working as a domestic worker. She visits me on her weekend off or on Thursdays. I'll find her at home maybe doing some washing for me, or ironing. So on Thursdays and the weekends I know she is coming to help me.

On the weekends I'm only free on Sundays. Saturdays I'm at classes. On Sundays I do work at home. Last year my husband didn't mind that I was studying. This year he complained.

He thinks maybe I'm becoming naughty here. Maybe I've got some boyfriends, or something. I don't know why he didn't want me to come to classes. But we quarrel about study. Sometimes when I'm studying he just comes and covers my books. He claims I'm concentrating too much on books.

One day he told me to stop going to classes. I didn't argue. I said, "Let it be my last Saturday today, and I'll tell Clive (the co-ordinator) that I am no longer coming." When I came to Clive I didn't say anything. But I told my husband that Clive said I must meet the seniors and explain to them.

On that very Saturday we were told that classes were cancelled for the next two weeks. So I just stayed at home on those Saturdays as if I was complying with the regulations of not going to classes.

Then one day when I came home from school I said, "Hm, you know what? The manager of Mobil, who's paying for us at Turret, has phoned me and said I must pay back their money because I've not been attending." Then my husband said, "How much do they want?" and I said, "More than R1 000." And he said, ''Oh I don't know how I'm going to get that money. By the way, how many months are you left with Turret?" And I told him it was only four or five months. And he said it was okay for me to go on. Ah well, I had to play that trick.

(Louise Yekwa was interviewed in June 1984.)

7

Organising women workers

So the truth began to dawn then how I keep him fit and trim
So the boss can make a nice fat profit out of me and him,
And as a solid union man he got in quite a rage
To think that we're both working hard and getting one man's wage,
I said 'And what about the part-time packing job I do?
That's three men that I work for, love, my boss, your boss, and you!'

He looked a little sheepish and he said 'As from today,
The lads and me will see what we can do on equal pay.
Would you like a housewives' union? Do you think you should be paid
As a cook and as a cleaner, as a nurse and as a maid?'
I said 'Don't jump the gun, love, if you did your share at home,
Perhaps I'd have some time to fight some battles of my own!'

As we have seen, women suffer great disadvantages at work and at home. The only solution to their many problems is for women to join together and fight for a better deal. But the task of organising women in trade unions and other organisations is also very difficult.

Farm and domestic workers

Chapter One showed that two thirds of black women workers are service and agricultural workers. These sectors are very difficult to organise. Many of these workers work on their own or in small groups for one employer. As individual workers they have little bargaining power. They are very vulnerable and are frequently fired or victimised by their employers. So it is difficult to bring these women together to discuss their problems and to work out ways of solving them.

Despite these problems there are growing numbers of organisations working with domestic workers. Margaret Nhlapo of SADWA (South African Domestic Workers Association) says:

"We do not offer many services, because domestic workers are not covered by any laws. But we are teaching domestic workers to speak for themselves. We are trying to show them — and the madams — what their labour is worth."

Transport and General Workers annual general meeting (Soweto, 1984)

Factory workers

Trade union work is easier among factory workers. But there are still relatively few women in the independent trade unions.

One important reason for this is that so many women workers are unskilled, and they are more likely to be fired if they become militant trade unionists. One trade union organiser said:

"Women have been brought into industry as unskilled labour. This means that they can easily be replaced, and they do not have much bargaining power — especially when unemployment is high."

The example on the opposite page shows how vulnerable women workers are.

A third shift

The majority of women workers struggle to find the time for trade union activity. Their jobs and their housework take up all their waking hours. Women who become active in trade unions are taking on a third shift! Also, many husbands do not like their wives going to union meetings after hours. This has become such a problem that some unions have special letters that women can take to their husbands, confirming meetings.

Lydia Kompe is the branch secretary of the Transport and General Workers Union. She explains why so many women drop out of the trade unions.

"They start to feel the pressures at home. Not only is it dangerous for a woman to attend meetings late at night, but she also knows that when she gets home she will find everything as she left it. Her husband will be sitting idle. And he might not believe she's been in a meeting — he will accuse her of going around. This makes her retreat. She doesn't want to lose her family for the union, even if she's committed to it. So the organisation becomes weakened."

So it seems that the problems that women have in the workplace (unskilled jobs) and at home (the double shift) prevent them from being active in trade unions.

Leadership problems

The women who manage to stay in the unions also have their problems. Often women are intimidated by men and do not participate. They don't feel able to become leaders. There have been cases of male trade unionists actively trying to keep women down. Sometimes women are not voted into leadership positions because women are not respected. Lydia Kompe says:

"Women have shown commitment in the trade unions, they have shown bravery. They have been active in the shop stewards' committees. We have got unions where the majority of members are women. But why have we not seen a woman chairperson of one of these unions? And where are the women presidents? And I don't expect the answer, 'It's because they're women.'"

The weak position of women in the trade union movement has important results. There is no

SOUTH AFRICAN FABRICS (PTY) LTD

SA Fabrics is a textile factory at Rossburgh in Durban. It is under the umbrella of Courtaulds, a British group of companies. This factory was first organised by NUTW in 1974, but the organisation collapsed in 1976, due to the Government's detention of Union leadership. It was re-organised in 1979.

The factory at that time had a total workforce of 600 male workers, of which about 60% were union members. Then in January 1980 the company started hiring and training female workers. These women were paid even less than half of what was paid to the male employees.

In mid-1980 there were already about 35 females in the plant, and the number was growing fast. The intention of the management was not only to fill the empty vacancies, but also to employ more workers at the cheapest possible prices. During October right up to December of that year, the Company and the Union were negotiating on two major issues, the first being the Procedural Agreement. What was important in that agreement was a clause which stated that the Union and the Company would try and solve disputes jointly, failing which the matter would then be referred to arbitration. This agreement was finalised and signed in 1981.

The second issue was the question of the January wage increase. Under this issue the workers were putting forward two demands:
1   a 15% increase of wages to all workers, and
2   that the company should "close" the discriminatory gap between male and female wages.

This issue came to a deadlock. The result was a 3-day strike in February 1981. After the strike, the two parties accepted arbitration as the only means of resolving the matter.

So while the Company was hiring the best lawyers in the country, the Union decided to bring Bro. Charles Ford, who is the General Secretary for I.T.G.L.W.F. (International Textile, Garment and Leather Workers Federation) to be present at the hearing. He gave evidence of what is happening in Courtaulds as far as women labour is concerned.

What happened after the arbitration is that the Judge's finding became very sweet to the Union, and very sour to the Company; the workers won 12½% increase, with 3 months' back pay; and the Company was ordered to close the wage gap between the male and female workers.

Thereafter the Company became so hostile to the workers that they started retrenchments. In those retrenchments most of the workers were women.

The Company has now only two female workers left from those who were employed during the big rush. One of those two workers has been saved because she is making tea for the big bosses. The other one is just there by sheer good luck.

(Signed)
SHOP STEWARD, SA FABRICS

women's voice which could make organisers and members aware of women workers' special problems. Frequently unions do not begin to tackle issues which affect women. So women stay in their weak positions in the workplace.

Recent gains

Recently this situation has begun to change. Women's groups are forming within the unions. Militant women organisers are making their voices heard. Trade unions have started negotiating with management on issues that specifically affect women.

One of these issues is maternity rights. In 1983 CCAWUSA (The Commercial Catering and Allied Workers Union) won a maternity agreement with the OK Bazaars. This allows women one year's maternity leave — without pay. The Sweet, Food and Allied Workers' Agreement with Kelloggs allows women three months paid maternity leave — but does not guarantee that they will get their jobs back.

In July 1984 there was an agreement between the Chemical Workers Industrial Union and NCS Plastics, which is the first to give women the right to paid maternity leave. This allows three months maternity leave, at one third pay, three months unpaid maternity leave and two days paternity leave. The employers also undertake to help women get their UIF benefit. Together with the UIF benefit, the maternity pay amounts to 78% of the normal wage.

These kinds of agreements are very new, and the victories are not yet big enough. But they are a step forward for black women workers.

Women trade unionists are determined to fight for women workers' rights. They realise that this is important for all workers. As Maggie Magubane, then general secretary of the Sweet, Food and Allied Workers Union said:

"We need to act now. For we don't want to wake up in years to come and find that women have been left behind in the struggle. We need to break down every division between men and women, by taking on the problems face to face. One thing is for sure — if we don't address the problems, the bosses will play the women off against the men."

A SADWA adminstrator discusses domestic worker's rights with SADWA members. (Johannesburg, 1984)

Some members of the Fosatu women's group: (L-R) Grace Monamodi, Refiloe Ndzuta, Liza Makalela, Maggie Magubane (Germiston, 1984)

Emma Mashinini talks to workers Naphtali Mokgoatsana and Mary Phaka.
(Johannesburg,1985)

Emma Mashinini

Emma Mashinini is general secretary of CCAWUSA (Commercial Catering and Allied Workers Union). She recalls her involvement from the early days when CCAWUSA had only two members. She talks about the problems which women workers in her union face.

I was working in the clothing industry for nearly twenty years before I was appointed to start at CCAWUSA. That was in 1974.

There were a lot of struggles at that time, really. It was my first time to work alone in an office. I had come from one of the largest factories in the clothing industry — with machines buzzing all the time and all that noise. And here I find myself in an office all by myself. I had a desk and furniture, but I didn't even have paper to write on. And it was too quiet for me. I was very cold. I used to shiver on the warmest day because it was too lonely!

I still remember our first two members. But the union has grown from strength to strength to where it is today. It's such a pleasure to see where the union is. I have very many able colleagues who are making the union a success.

At the moment the membership is over forty thousand. The majority of our members are in the supermarkets. It's about 50/50, men and women. In the supermarkets and the stores the women outnumber the men, but the men make up at the warehouses.

Up until a year ago there were equal numbers of men and women on our executive (six men, six women). But we had our elections and now there are eight men and four women. But who's responsible for that? It's the women themselves. I don't know why. It's the women who will always elect a man.

Why? What deceives them? Because when we are in meetings the women are more outspoken than men. And with the strikes, you find that the people who've actually worked very hard to see that the strike comes into being — it's the women. And for the strike to be a success — it's the women. And when it's negotiated and it's time to go back to work, or whatever — the people who opt for it are the women. Women are at the forefront of everything...and the men co-operate.

Also, when we have our seminars we have a good number of women attending. And they make good teachers as well. But there are problems with anything that keeps them away from home overnight and so forth. It does seem to be the partner at home who is not in favour of them being in the union.

Only this morning a certain gentleman walks in: "I've come to enquire about my wife who wrote to you six months ago that she wants to resign from the union. But each time I look at her payslip there's a union deduction on it." But neither I nor my colleagues could remember receiving that letter. Now, what clearly dawned on me is this. This lady wants to be a union member — but her husband objects. And this lady, just to protect herself, must have said, "I've written a letter and they continue." So who doesn't want to be a union member? It is this man. But I'm sure he's a member of a football club.

At work women also have problems. Especially when it comes to promotion. Black women are being left behind. In fact women as a whole are the last ones to be promoted. You are promoted for being a white man before you are promoted for being a white women. But given a choice of the two (groups of women), the black one is at the bottom of the ladder.

We have made a lot of progress since our first maternity agreement with OK Bazaars in 1983. I think we have maternity agreements with every company we had a recognition agreement with. It's a big help, I must say. Especially now that the workers are sure to get their jobs back after maternity leave.

And what is worse, before these maternity agreements you were dismissed as soon as you were noticeable. Or you were victimized for being expectant. You were removed from the front because you were an ugly sight. You had to go into the back — into the storerooms and so forth. And it's heavier work as well.

And afterwards when you wanted your job back, you had to go every day to say "I'm ready, I'm ready". Until you're tired. And some managers would just say, "We have filled your vacancy — and that's that." You have nowhere to go.

And when a woman with long service went on maternity it was considered broken service. When she came back it affected her wages and everything. She had to start from down below. And when it comes to retrenchment you're last in.

It's all changed with these agreements. You get the same salary when you come back from leave. And if there's a statutory increase — like the wage board — while you were away, you are going to get it. Also we are getting time off for mothers to look after sick babies and have a check-up themselves.

Now we have been fighting retrenchments in OK Bazaars. It's so upsetting because they are creating key positions to protect certain people. This helps them get around the LIFO (last in, first out) system. It is mainly white people in these key posts. With no training nê? When you argue about these key posts with no training they say, "You don't know his background." That's our South Africa for you.

We negotiated these retrenchments together with NUDAW (the union which organises white workers). And they fought equally with us. But we have pointed out that there is no equality on the shop floor between our members and theirs.

You know, when we heard that there are going to be retrenchments in OK Bazaars nobody knew who was going to be retrenched — black and white. The shop stewards were telling us they are all standing together and they are consulting one another. They see themselves as one because there is this problem hanging over them.

Some time ago there was a strike in Checkers over the demotion of a white woman. The workers said it was an unfair demotion of a colleague of theirs — they didn't see it as a white woman being demoted. And they went out on strike. And she got her previous job back.

It seems we have to have problems to get together and be one, and equal. When it is good times then certain workers are superior to others.

It is the first time that CCAWUSA has been so hard hit by retrenchments. We haven't had retrenchments like our colleagues in industry have experienced. But it's going to get worse.

It's very very tough to be out of a job. I don't know what those people are going to do to survive. It's not right to retrench women first. The family suffers as much if the woman is out of a job. Because you know, compared to men we are the ones who keep the homes going. Of course it's important for us that our men should keep their jobs,

Alan Fine

'An injury to one is an injury to all' say these Checkers workers.
In 1983 they went on strike because a (white) worker was demoted. (Germiston, 1983)

because they are seen as heads of the households. I qualify to have a home because I am a married woman. And if the man is out of a job sooner or later we will be having no home.

So it's equally important for men to keep their jobs − instead of management making use of child labour. Because they spend money on casuals − who most of the time are youngsters − and comfortable white children at that.

Why must they use children when there is a parent who needs a job? That child, when he gets his pay he's going to buy a BMX. He doesn't have to worry about rent and school books to be paid. Maybe he's got that job because his dad is managing something and he wants a school holiday job. There's no need for it.

(Emma Mashinini was interviewed in January 1985.)

Mam' Lydia Kompe,
trade unionist — at home

— at work

Mam' Lydia

Lydia Kompe is branch secretary of the Transport and General Workers Union. She talks about some of the problems of women trade unionists.

After I became a shop steward at MAWU we had a lot of meetings, maybe twice a week. My husband used to expect me home between 5.30 p.m. and 6 p.m. But sometimes I wouldn't even go home because we'd have meetings at our centre in Tembisa, and I was living in Alexandra. Sometimes it was too late to go home, and I'd sleep with friends.

This made my husband very unhappy and it made our life miserable. He couldn't see why I was involved in this. He was scared I'd be in politics and land in jail. He'd get very unhappy and think I was making excuses about meetings when I was going out jolling. When we got dismissed it was worse because he felt I deserved it.

I tried to explain to him — and encourage him to organise at his place. He was a worker at a laboratory in Jeppe. But they had no union.

You know what husbands are like. He'd complain that I didn't do anything for him — cook, make tea or do the washing. It's true that I preferred to do the washing at night rather than miss any meetings. I'd rather strain and overwork at night to satisfy him. But he wasn't happy and said that wasn't the answer. He needed me to be with him. But he couldn't put me off because I felt it was important to carry on. Now he's got used to it and he doesn't worry me so much. He's getting old.

That's the problem with married women in the organisation. You're in the middle and don't know what to do. Even at work if you think of the problems at home you don't concentrate — you find yourself getting depressed. What will you find at home? What attitude will you get from your husband, even your children?

At one and the same time you have to have a job, be in the union and run the home. If you're a young woman maybe there's also a baby to look after. Maybe in the mornings you take your child to a creche or to an old woman. If the man comes home early he hasn't the ability to go and fetch the child and look after it while you're working. He expects the woman to go and fetch the baby, put it behind her back, get to the stove and cook for him — and he's busy reading the paper.

And we do it happily because we grew up that way, we saw our parents do it and we think it's the African way.

Women also have problems in the unions. At Heinemann we had six women shop stewards out of twelve. This was because we were insisting, and our organiser, Khubeka, was encouraging us. But our chairperson was still a man.

During meetings we tried to fight the undermining of women's suggestions. They thought we were not saying strategic things. But we managed to fight that. We succeeded in Heinemann because, as I said, women outnumbered men. The women were taking the lead when we were on strike. They weren't scared even when the police were trying to thrash us and scare us with dogs. I think that's when the women realised that women can be determined.

But now we have some women shop stewards from Anglo and even though they are not taking the lead they're actually participating quite well. I don't

know if it's perhaps because these men have been organised by me that they give them respect.

There are now a lot of women in FOSATU (Federation of South African Trade Unions). But no union has yet elected a branch chairlady. Perhaps a female treasurer, since people think a woman is more responsible and will be more careful with the money.

Even the women feel it's more important to elect men. I don't know why.

I think it's time for women to come together and see that this thing is a major problem for us. So that

eventually we achieve the same rights. And we must think of many ways of doing it. It's a problem that will go ahead from one generation to another if we don't actually work on it now.

(Lydia Kompe was interviewed in 1983.)

Transport and General Workers Union
annual general meeting –
the leadership and the members
(Morena Stores, Katlehong, 1982)

Liza Makalela

Liza is the administrator for NAAWU (National Automobile and Allied Workers Union). She talks about the way the (male) organisers relate to her – as an administrator and as a woman.

I do typing and filing, I write out cheques for the sick fund benefits, attend to the telephone, attend to people coming in. Maybe if there's a general meeting, hire buses and all that. It's such a lot of work, you can't even cope.

I am not treated as an equal by the others, though I am fighting for that, day and night. They don't report things to me or tell me where they are going. They don't discuss union matters with me. If I object to whatever is happening, they'll change for a few minutes, and then go back to the same attitude of putting me in my place. Most of the men are like that, but not all of them.

I am sometimes included in union decision-making. As long as we have a meeting in the office, no problem, I'm included. In fact I forced my way into that because constitutionally administrators are not delegates to any meetings.

What I have noticed is that if I am not present at a meeting they do not record my apology in the minutes. But when I'm there they do include my name. The organisers told me I must be present when there is a finance meeting because I have to answer queries.

I can't say I don't feel a full part of the union – because I want to be. At some stage they'll be forced to take it into consideration.

Attitudes have improved since I've been here – simply because I have fought it. I retaliate every time when there is something I don't like. And I am so used to it – it doesn't humiliate me any more.

They used to ask me to make tea, but now I refuse. I only make tea if I feel I should do it. If, for instance, we are having a meeting with management in the office, I do make tea.

And even cleaning – I thought we all should do it. But they said, "You are a woman, it's your job." I felt, no man, I didn't come here for cleaning. So I stopped.

I am part of this FOSATU women's group. It started in 1983 after the FOSATU education workshop. They decided to have a programme on women workers. It was just a quick thing, and then it was presented for all the workers. The hall was full. But what those women presented was . . . well, what people understood was that these women were complaining about housework, and about being controlled by men, and so on. The thing was not so clear, and it was dismissed by many people.

Afterwards we met and we thought about it. We decided to drop the whole double shift thing and now try to concentrate on a woman at work. We started compiling a booklet.

After that we drafted a model maternity agreement. We even called a big general meeting, and a lot of women responded – here in Rosslyn. Together we drafted the agreement. The agreement said that jobs must be guaranteed back and we demanded pay for six months, and unpaid leave for another six months.

Up until now we have not been able to get paid leave — at least not for six months. Management goes according to the ordinary law where they say maternity leave should be three months. But at least it's better than before, because they just used to dismiss pregnant workers.

But we've never got what we want in that model agreement, no.

A weakness is that most of the time it's been negotiated by men, you see. They do not talk from experience, and I don't think it's deep down in their hearts. Because most men feel that a woman shouldn't work.

And sometimes these men complain that women are taking their jobs — and women are paid less, that's why they are in. But it's not true in the motor industry. Now they pay them equally.

During maternity negotiations management said, "No, no, if women are going to be so expensive we'd better not have them here, because they're not so useful to us. We can't afford to pay them maternity."

I would like to remind management that women are going to have children who will be tomorrow's workers. Management must contribute to that, because they are paying low wages. We cannot afford to stay at home to look after the children. We must go back to work. We must be given a chance.

But management says, "It's your business, if you want to have children, you can have your children, and you must stay at home. If you want to work, you must work."

I've got four kids at home. I'm living with my mother. I'm not married — I'm used to this single life. My children understand that I'm working, and I'm alone. If they want something that I can't give them, they understand why.

I can't say any of my children came by mistake because I wanted to have them, though I don't want a husband. I wouldn't cope now, it would be too much.

I experience problems now with my boyfriend. He says, "Jrr, I wish I had married you. I can't sit here and wait for a woman to come home at ten o'clock. And you are with a lot of men the whole day, and I don't know what is happening . . . ." This and that, you see.

If I was married it would be hard for me to do this job. I'm not ready to go and sit at home — there's a lot of work to be done.

(Liza Makalela was interviewed in September 1984.)

DEMANDS

In February 1984 the National Automobile and Allied Workers Union presented a paper on women workers to management at AECI. These were their demands.

1 The employer should ensure that all employees are paid the rate for the job. No wages should fall below a living wage of R3,50 per hour.

2 No overtime should be compulsory — compulsory overtime means three shifts. This does not mean all women do not want to do overtime — they may need the money just like the men. Women are not all in the same position. Overtime should be voluntary, not compulsory.

3 Employers should ensure that sexual harassment is not condoned. If it occurs then disciplinary action should follow immediately.

4 Employers should realise that women do a double shift — at home and at work, and that she is continually torn between employer and family. These problems should constitute valid reasons in disciplinary hearings.

5 Employers should give low interest loans to all employees to help them buy electricity for their homes. Workers should not be expected to put down a deposit because low wages mean they cannot afford these. It costs R700 to install lights and plugs — it costs much more for geysers.

Maternity

1 Education on contraception, to be given by a person acceptable to workers.

2 Family planning clinics should be equipped with a full range of contraceptives so that women workers have a genuine right to choose the contraceptive that is best for them.

3 Women should be given the right to attend ante- and post-natal clinics without loss of pay.

4 Women should be given the right to maternity leave and to return to the same or a similar position after such leave.

5 Women should be given the right to full pay while on maternity leave.

Child care

1 We need to have nurseries. Employers should accept collective responsibility for providing facilities for child care. They cannot hide behind the government's failure to provide these facilities. It will be advantageous for employers because it will reduce the number of absentees due to child care responsibility.

2 Recreational facilities or youth centres for young people can be useful for youngsters to use their free time constructively.

I wouldn't like my child to grow the same way as I did,
or to be as I am now. I would like my grandchildren to actually feel free —
in organisations, at home, everywhere. They should have the same say,
the same rights.

Mam' Lydia Kompe, trade unionist

Acknowledgements

We would like to thank all the people who have contributed to this book.

Resource material: Joanne Yawitch

Interview contributions: Jeremy Baskin (Mam' Lydia), Aninka Claasens (Alice, Anna, Rose Modise), Mary Anne Cullinan (Mildred Mjekula), Baby Tyawa (Agnes Thulare), Joanne Yawitch (Rose).

Translations: Aninka Claasens, Mothibi Mthetwa, Elizabeth Tshayinca

Typing: Duchenne Werren

Thanks also to the following for their advice, information and practical help: Jane Barrett, Adrienne Bird, Pam Christie, Jackie Cock, Fosatu Women's Study Group, Pamela Greet, Goodman Mabote, Margaret Nhlapo, Annah Phalime, Nellie Robertson, Nick Swann National Automobile and Allied Workers Union

Organisations offering assistance to workers

A short list of organisations which offer assistance to women workers is available from Ravan Press. The list includes trade unions, organisations working in rural areas, domestic worker associations, legal clinics, etc. If you would like a copy of this list, write to Ravan Press, P O Box 31134, Braamfontein, 2017 South Africa.

Sources

Barrett J, "Knitmore. A study in the relationship between sex and class." Honours thesis, University of the Witwatersrand, Johannesburg, 1981.

Baskin J, "Women and Trade Unions." *South African Labour Bulletin* Vol 8, No 6, 1983.

Beale J, *Getting it together: Women as trade unionists*. Pluto Press. London, 1982.

Bird A, "Organising women in South Africa. Trade Unions". Unpublished paper, 1983.

Biscuit Manufacturing Industrial Council Agreement No R2301, October 30, 1981.

Bohardien G, Lehulere K, Shaw A, *Domestic workers and poverty*. Second Carnegie Commission on Poverty and Development in South Africa. Cape Town, 1984.

Cock J, Emdon E, Klugman B, *Childcare and the working mother*. Second Carnegie Commission on Poverty and Development in South Africa. Cape Town, 1984.

Department of Statistics, *South African Statistics*. Pretoria, 1980.

De Klerk M, *Farm wages in the western Transvaal*. Second Carnegie Commission on Poverty and Development in South Africa. Cape Town, 1984.

Farm Labour Project, *Submission to Manpower Commission on farm labour*. Johannesburg, 1983.

Favis M, "Black women in the South African economy." Unpublished paper, 1983.

Fosatu Education, *Women Workers*. Fosatu Printing Unit. Durban, 1984.

Fosatu Education Workshop, Unpublished papers on women workers. Germiston, 1983.

Hirsh A, "An introduction to textile worker organisation in Natal." *South African Labour Bulletin* Vol 4, No 8, 1979.

Horner D B, Budlender D, Hendrie D, Young R G, *Industrial Council wage rates and poverty*. Second Carnegie Commission on Poverty and Development in South Africa. Cape Town, 1984.

Kerr S, "The Maintenance Engineer." Published in *My Song is My Own*. Kathy Henderson, Frankie Armstrong, Sandra Kerr (eds). Pluto Press, 1979.

Manotti A M, "The incorporation of African Women into wage employment in South Africa 1920-1970." PhD Dissertation, University of Connecticut, 1980.

National Automobile and Allied Workers Union, *Women at Work*. Fosatu Printing Unit. Durban, 1984.

South African Institute of Race Relations, *Survey of Race Relations*, 1964, 1982, 1983. Johannesburg.

South African Research Services, *South African Review No 1: Same Foundations, New Facades*. Ravan Press. Johannesburg, 1983.

Trades Union Congress, *Working Women*. TUC. College Hill Press (TUC), 1983.

Yawitch J, "The relation between African female employment and influx control in South Africa 1950 -1983." MA Dissertation, University of Witwatersrand, Johannesburg, 1984.